How to Self Publish

A Bestseller's Guide to Self-publishing

(Step-by Step Picture Guide on How to Write and Publish Your Books)

Donald Jones

Published By **Region Loviusher**

Donald Jones

How to Self Publish: A Bestseller's Guide to Self-publishing (Step-by Step Picture Guide on How to Write and Publish Your Books)

ISBN   978-1-998038-24-4

Legal & Disclaimer

Table Of Contents

Chapter 1: Why Am I Writing This Book?

Hack 1 on this step-with the aid of the usage of-step guide is to mirror on what's crucial to you. What are you obsessed with? What lifestyles reminiscences form who you are today? What do you need to perform with the aid of the use of writing your e-book? You are the author. Hack 1 permits you find out the e-book topics that incredible fit who you're.

This is essential on numerous ranges. First, if you write a ebook on a subject you discover stupid, maximum in all likelihood it's miles going to be tough to complete. If you don't care approximately the undertaking, you won't be capable of do the paintings it takes to get it out to the general public. Knowing who you are and why you're writing this e-book will assist you advantage the courage and stamina it will take to get the procedure finished.

Here are the motion elements for Hack 1:

•Create a listing of the happiest instances in your lifestyles

•Make a few one-of-a-kind listing of the saddest times on your lifestyles

•Create some other listing of different jobs and pastimes you revel in

•Fill in the table on the cease of those commands. In the primary column, listing 10 characteristics that describe your first-class lifestyles. These can be such things as glad, sincere, loving, famous, reliable, and so on.

•In the second one column, listing 10 successes you want to perform for your life. These can be such things as write 5 books, be an fantastic dad or mum, climb Mount Everest, and masses of others.

•In the 0.33 column, list 10 possessions you want to enjoy in your lifestyles. These gadgets would likely consist of a brand new residence, a racecar, a cabin inside the woods, or technology device, and many others.

#	BE	DO	HAVE	HELP
1				
2				
3				
4				
5				
6				
7				
8				
9				
10				

In the fourth column, listing 10 organizations or groups you need to assist to your existence. These is probably companies like your circle of relatives, awful youngsters in Nigeria, the America Red Cross, and so forth.

•When you fill within the lists, positioned an asterisk beside the three gadgets in each column which might be the most vital to you.

Just a phrase of warning proper proper right here. You can be tempted to skip the bodily games as we undergo the guide. Please don't! None of the stairs is difficult to do, however every one is critical and want to be completed within the order I present them. Trust me. I needed to go into reverse commonly and wasted heaps of time. Follow the plan and also you obtained't make the equal mistakes!

You completed the primary hack. Congratulations! You are for your manner to writing and publishing a bestselling Kindle e-book!

WHAT IS THE BEST KINDLE CATEGORY FOR MY BOOK?

Hack 2 is to exercising session which ebook you will write. If you check the checklists we did in Hack 1, you wrote many suitable thoughts approximately the e-book you want to write down. The fantastic books come from authors with enjoy concerning a selected trouble who supply assist and answers to others in similar situations.

What we need to do in Hack 2 is assist you find out the amazing instructions in which to put in writing your eBook. You want to choose out training humans are inquisitive about and already buying books. The high-quality manner to do this is to use Amazon Kindle to do magnificence research. I'll guide you through this step-by manner of the usage of-step so you apprehend what to do:

•Go to Amazon. Com. Make certain you are not signed into your Amazon account due to the truth this will exchange the consequences based totally on books you purchased in the beyond.

•Choose KINDLE STORE on the trying to find bar.

•Enter "Kindle" within the are looking for bar and select out GO. This will deliver up the top selling books inside the Amazon store.

•Choose KINDLE EBOOKS at the left navigation bar (You may additionally moreover furthermore need to select + SEE MORE).

•Create a spreadsheet with the subsequent columns: 'Category Name', '1st Book Sale's Rank', 'fifth Book Sale's Rank', 'tenth Book Sale's Rank', 'twentieth Book Sale's Rank', and 'Use Category?'

•Work thru the types and subcategories on the left navigation pane and pick out ones you're interested by writing a e book approximately. I use the "Format as Table" characteristic in Excel to kind and study the information without problem. Choose the types or subcategories which is probably actual opportunities.

•Fill inside the following records for classes or subcategories you choose out: Category Name, 1st Book Sales Rank, 5th Book Sales Rank, 10th Book Sales Rank, and 20th Book Sales Rank. The Book Sales Rank is placed midway down the e-book's internet web page. I right click on the ebook's photograph and select out "Open in a New Tab." That makes it a good deal less tough to undergo the list.

•After you fill out the spreadsheet, type the books via the use of "1st Book Sales Rank." For any training with a "1st Book Sales Rank" extra than 7,500 positioned "No" inside the "Use Category?" column.

•Sort the books with the aid of manner of the usage of "5th Book Sales Rank." Enter "No" within the "Use Category?" column if the fifth Book Sales Rank is more than 15,000.

•Sort the books by way of the usage of "10th Book Sales Rank." Enter "No" within the "Use Category?" column if the 5th Book Sales Rank is extra than 30,000.

•Sort the books with the beneficial resource of "twentieth Book Sales Rank." Enter "No" within the "Use Category?" column if the fifth Book Sales Rank is more than 60,000.

•Enter "Yes" in every "Use Category?" row that doesn't have "No." The last classes are the only to goal at the same time as you write your ebook. You can write a ebook in a few detail elegance you need, but the schooling in this listing embody the subjects people are interested by purchasing for.

•Draw the following image and fill it in with material from Steps 1 and multiple:

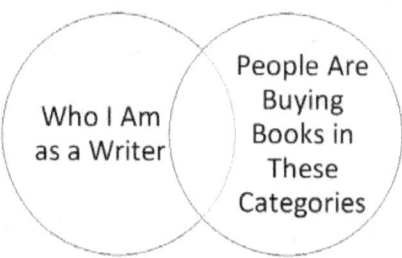

Now take time to suppose through the segment inside the middle — how do the "who you're" and "what training human beings are searching for books for" overlap? Then, fill within the middle phase the use of this template: I pick out out the _____ category because of the fact _____ (Who I Am).

•Make positive the "commands" and developments of "who you're as a author" overlap.

•Put a celeb beside the three categories within the middle which is probably most exciting and interesting to you whilst you recall writing a e-book.

•Software Alert! I use KINDLE SPY to do the magnificence, task be counted range, micro-problem count number, and keyword research fast. Full Disclosure – I acquire a small referral rate if you pick out out the link. My referral does no longer increase your software utility rate if you choose out to shop for Kindle Spy and you may find out the software by way of the usage of way of looking for it on Google.

And that's it for Hack 2: What is the Best Book Category for Me?

Chapter 2: What Topic Should I Write About?

In Hack 3, we are succesful to walk through the steps to help you slim down which challenge depend is the superb one for your Kindle bestseller. Like the preceding Hack, we want to find out which topics human beings are interested in and already searching out. This modifications over time, however your e-book has the incredible threat of promoting nicely if it addresses a topic that people are interested by shopping for correct now.

Maybe you have got a subject already and don't want to "discover a topic." That's quality. I want you to undergo this exercise to get mind to reinforce your present day-day book or locate the challenge on your next one. The following exercise will help you popularity your ebook scenario matter and this lets in in reading, writing, and advertising.

So right here are the motion points for Hack three: What Topic Should I Write About?

•Open a phrase processing report and make contact with it "Book Topic Research – [Month] [Year]." Change the month and yr to a few element they're for you currently.

•Go to Amazon.Com in your internet browser. Make positive you signed from your Amazon account so in advance purchases you've got made don't have an impact at the quest consequences.

•Choose KINDLE STORE from the menu, followed thru "Best Sellers" and then pick out GO.

•Choose TOP a hundred KINDLE EBOOKS underneath the hunt bar.

•Choose KINDLE EBOOKS in the left navigation bar.

•Navigate to one of the final education you selected on the end of the second step.

•Select all of the books the usage of your mouse. You do now not need to replicate the classified ads and promotions on the net net web page or it's going to make the following steps greater tough. (It works higher if you start from the bottom of the books and art work your manner to the top). Use Ctrl + C to duplicate as soon as you have got the books decided on.

•Paste the outcomes in your word file the use of the "Plain Text" fashion.

•Go to the lowest of the internet page, spotlight books 21-forty, and repeat the previous movement factors.

•Repeat the sooner motion steps for books 41-60.

•Go in your phrase file and replica the complete file thru the use of choosing Ctrl + A after which Ctrl + C.

•Go to WriteWords.Org

•Paste (Ctrl + V) the whole lot within the "Paste Your Text" box. Choose "2" as range of phrases in a phrase.

•Think thru the results and file any -word terms which are fantastic viable topics.

•Do the previous 4 steps, changing the "phrases in a phrase" to "three," then "four," then "5," after which "6." Mix and rearrange the wording till you have at least ten topics.

•Do the ones motion elements for each of the 3 instructions you chose in Hack 2.

•Place your lists of subjects within the "Possible Topics" circle internal the instance.

Now, take time to think about the section within the middle – how "who you are" and "subjects humans are shopping for books about" overlaps. Then fill inside the center section as follows: I select the _____ concern don't forget because _____ (Who I Am). Make nice the "topics" and traits of "who you're as a writer" surely overlap.

•Star three topics in the middle wherein the circles overlap that make you pound the desk with ardour or satisfaction.

•Book Alert! If you want greater statistics in this hack, I endorse Steve Scott's ebook known as:

•How to Get Best-Selling Nonfiction Ebook Ideas

And that's the cease of Hack 3! I understand this step takes time and you can marvel, "When will I begin writing the ebook?" Laying a stable foundation takes time and paintings that humans in no way see. Be confident, this artwork can pay off and provide you with the studies you need to put in writing down numerous books for your subject matter (area of hobby).

WHAT IS THE BEST MICRO-TOPIC FOR MY BOOK?

Let's evaluate the development you've got got made thus far.

In Hack 1, we did a few soul-looking: what you experience and what you dislike. Life evaluations which have formed you. What your goals, goals, and passions are. You have to write many books, however Hack 1 narrowed the sphere to topics you may be an professional on – the most important key to a robust non-fiction ebook.

In Hack 2, we looked at which instructions are promoting the most books. Amazon is your great pal for marketplace research. Amazon offers updated information in actual time. Authors and publishers inside the past gave masses of cash for this data, and it was at the least 90 days antique. You get it loose. You then in evaluation those classes to your passions, studies, and desires. The result modified right into a listing of training you may write in and be confident you may promote books.

Researching a class that human beings are inquisitive about and that sells books is not sufficient, despite the truth that. In Hack three, you narrowed the sector in addition with the useful resource of manner of uncovering which subjects in that elegance have been selling the great. Topics sell because human beings are interested in them today. The top records is that human beings are looking for books nowadays. When you write a e-book people are inquisitive about, it's going to sell.

Now we are at Hack four. In this step, we are able to pick out in reality taken into consideration one in every of your three topics and do more marketplace studies on a trouble you could help people resolve inside that subject depend. Your purpose is to put in writing down a 15,000-word eBook that addresses that hassle and offers a smooth solution. When you end your studies, you may be assured you have got a micro-topic in case you want to help humans and they may want to shop for.

Picking a micro-subject matter will make your research and writing skip lots faster.

The terms will fly off your fingertips! You may have more authority because of the reality you are solving part of the large trouble and no longer everything. People looking for answers will discover your e-book a bargain a good deal less complicated due to the truth you have got centered your venture depend. After completing, you will be capable of write severa books on this problem remember or area of interest – any other key to doing well on Amazon.

So permit's get started out on Hack four: What is the Best Micro-Topic for My Book?

Follow the ones steps to do your research:

•Open a phrase processing record and communicate to it "Book Micro-Topic Research – [Month] [Year]." Change the month and year to something they are for you currently.

•You placed a celebrity beside 3 topics in Hack 3. All of those are capability bestselling subjects. You want to select out one in each of them now. After you write a ebook in that topic, you can write some unique bestselling ebook in one of the remaining topics. For now, despite the fact that, you want to select one. Pick your chosen!

•Go to Amazon.Com for your net browser. Make certain you signed from your Amazon account so earlier purchases you made do not have an effect on the are trying to find effects.

•Choose KINDLE STORE from the menu, input "Your Topic" and pick GO.

•Make first rate SORT BY: is set to "Relevance."

•Go to the number one ebook on the list. Use the LOOK INSIDE feature and open the book to the desk of contents.

•Type the table of contents of the ebook into the word processing document.

•Repeat the preceding steps for the top ten books within the are looking for for listing.

•Go on your phrase file and duplicate the complete report through choosing Ctrl + A after which Ctrl + C.

•Go to WriteWords.Org

•Paste (Ctrl + V) the entirety within the "Paste Your Text" region. Choose "2" as form of phrases in a phrase.

•Scan via the results and list any phrases with phrases that hobby you.

•Do the preceding 4 steps converting the "terms in a word" to a few, then four, then 5, then 6. Mix and rearrange the wording into at the least eight micro-subjects. These micro-subjects must be the pinnacle contenders.

•Each of the micro-topics you researched is the solution to a hassle. What we're interested in doing proper right here is locating what the trouble is. Spend time thinking through the micro-subject matter answer and expand a question that receives at the trouble. For instance, if the micro-topic is "come to be an active listener," then the problem question might be "How can I concentrate to others higher?"

•Create a double-elimination subject matter occasion the use of the 8 questions you developed in the previous step. Choose the winner in every bracket based definitely totally on how vital that query is to you and the humans you understand. Put as many stars as you need beside the winner.

•Celebrate! You have determined a micro-problem depend that have to serve you properly as a creator and writer.

•Software Alert – I use Better Book Tools to do that hack brief. Not only does Better Book Tools assist decide which micro-subject matter to pick, however the tremendous elegance and difficulty count variety from earlier Hacks. Full disclosure: I reap a small referral fee if you pick out out out the link. My referral does no longer boom your software software fee if you buy Better Book Tools and you can discover the software program application through looking for it on Google. I use each Kindle Spy and Better Book Tools due to the fact every tool embody extraordinary beneficial features.

And that's Hack 4. It took a while, but I promise you that having a focused micro hassle this is so important to humans is really well worth its weight in gold. Sorry for the cliché!

The foundation of your ebook is in area, now we bypass to the building detail. This is lots greater amusing for my part, but we can be confident the foundation will keep! So many books live unpublished due to a defective basis. Your e book won't be actually considered one of them.

Chapter 3: What Keywords Should I Use?

Hack five will help you locate the right key phrases on your book. A word of warning: you could spend loads of time doing this and enjoy the regulation of diminishing returns.

I understand what I am speaking approximately right here. Finding the proper key-word has been one quest on which I spent an excessive amount of time! At the surrender of this step, I will provide you with a listing of software program software tools that might keep time. But you have got been warned. Don't spend an excessive amount of time in this Hack!

The important search engines like google like google and yahoo – Google and Bing – depend on key phrases to assist searchers find what they want. Amazon and YouTube art work the identical way. What we need to do in Hack 5 is discover which key phrases humans are entering into the search engines like google like google to find out your e-book. Pure and clean.

The motive key terms are so vital is that the Internet is crammed complete of information, internet web sites, books, motion photographs, audio documents, and the list is developing. There are billions of pages. Without the search engines like google, finding the records you want on the Internet might be not possible. Each are searching out engine, as a quit result, uses key-phrase technology.

When you enter terms within the search bar of any are seeking out engine, their software program program software program tries to fit the phrases you entered with key terms that people entered for their net website on-line, e-book, and masses of others. The are in search of engine produces a listing of these net websites and tracks how many human beings click on on on each link. As buyers pick out out entries, the hunt engine marks them as greater applicable, and they show up higher in the autosuggestion of the search bars.

Entries which might be selected less regularly show up on later pages. Most folks who purchase a few element on the net click on on one of the first ten gadgets that come up in the are looking for engine results. This hack will assist you be one of the pinnacle ten!

Here are the steps for Hack 5: What Keywords Should I Use?

PART I – Finding Keywords

•Open a spreadsheet file and name it "Book Keyword Research – [Month] [Year]." Change the month and 12 months as appropriate.

•Go to Amazon.Com on your net browser. Make nice you signed from your Amazon account so in advance purchases you made will no longer have an effect on the seek effects.

•Choose KINDLE STORE from the menu.

•Take your micro-topic query and create a list of the nouns and verbs in the question. Record the ones inside the first column of the spreadsheet.

•If the noun is singular, add a plural to the list, and vice versa. Add the beyond demanding and present disturbing of every of the verbs to the list within the first column.

•Take each key-phrase on your list and enter the word into the Amazon are searching out bar one letter at a time. After you type a letter, see if any autosuggestion effects seem which might be associated with your problem matter. Record any new terms or terms in the very last column of your spreadsheet.

•Repeat the preceding steps until you cover each word (and new words) on the listing.

•Go to Google.Com on your net browser.

•Take the listing you advanced for Amazon.Com and repeat the gadget. Write any new phrases you discover at the lowest of the list. If a keyword or key-word word is on each Amazon and Google, make the word BOLD and boom its font duration so that you can effortlessly discover it.

•Return to Amazon.Com and enter any new terms you located at Google.Com. Enter each phrase a letter at a time and file new autosuggestion terms at the bottom of your key-word listing.

•Repeat the preceding six steps until no new autosuggestion terms appear.

Part 2: Finding the Best Keywords

•Create each different column inside the spreadsheet known as "Keystrokes."

•Enter each phrase or word, one letter at a time, within the Amazon.Com are searching for bar. When the key-word or word you're searching out suggests up inside the autosuggestion bar, report what number of letters (keystrokes) you entered. Often, a phrase or phrase will seem in the autosuggestion bar earlier than you kind within the complete phrase. We want to understand how swiftly the word appeared.

•When you have were given entered the substantial sort of keystrokes for every word and word, type the keystrokes column (lowest to maximum). Change the font color of the number one twenty phrases to RED.

•The first rate key terms so that you can use in this ebook are in RED and BOLD. Runner-up keywords are in RED. Third region keywords are in BLACK and BOLD. Last location key terms to use are in BLACK.

•Software Alert! Use SOOLVE.COM to do the heavy lifting on this hack. It is free and suggests you autosuggestion effects from Amazon, Google, Bing, and one-of-a-kind are searching for engine websites.

•Book Alert! If you want more facts on key-phrase studies, I recommend Chris Naish's book CreateSpace and Kindle Self-Publishing Matrix.

Hack 5 is within the bag! If you are like me, subjects have turn out to be a laugh now. Keyword research is so fascinating!

Heed the warning of a person who has traveled too long at the are searching for engine advertising course, but.

Complete the steps above and flow into immediately to the following hack. You can beautify on keywords after publishing your e-book, but the ones you've got had been given now will help your e-book promote well. Don't spend an excessive amount of time in this hack. You may additionally never placed up your e-book!

HOW TO CREATE A BESTSELLING TITLE & SUBTITLE

Hack 6 will help you expand a top notch title, subtitle, and series find out for your ebook. Keywords you discovered in your studies will help you develop a discover that connect people searching out your book topic. Your subtitle offers a small description on the manner to confirm or deny their perception of your ebook. A series name is some other way you can rank properly for keywords and start your publishing empire.

Hack 6 is essential because of the truth Amazon uses your pick out first to rank your e-book. If your pick out is unsure, readers will no longer take a hazard on what you are offering. A call that doesn't describe your e-book correctly can bring about poor critiques from readers.

Your name and subtitle are a compass to your writing. Follow the compass and you could get to your excursion spot!

Here are the movement steps for Hack 6: How to Create a Bestselling Title & Subtitle:

•Describe your e-book in a single word.

•Write one sentence that describes the principle point of your e book.

•Write a quick paragraph (at the least 5 sentences) describing the hassle and answer your e book tackles.

•Look at your list of key terms from Hack five. Choose the RED and BOLD key-phrase or key-word word that has the least keystrokes earlier than performing in the Amazon autosuggestion pane.

•Create a call that makes use of the important thing-word or a key phrase inside the final step. Begin the call with this key-word or word. For instance, Write and Publish a Book, become the primary RED and BOLD key-phrase word for this e-book. So, "Write and Publish a Book" come first in my call. The find out need to describe or allude to the trouble people are seeking to treatment.

•Create a subtitle that uses the second one key-phrase or phrase this is RED and BOLD. The subtitle must encompass or allude to the solution the problem that the name facts.

•Create a sequence come to be privy to the usage of RED and BOLD key-word huge range three for your key-phrase word listing. Create a chain name that ends with the phrases "guide" or "guide." The collection perceive have to encompass room for destiny books you write.

•Creating a name, subtitle, and series name is both an art work and a technological know-how. The key phrases you researched come up with the "technological facts" part of growing them. Now you have to use your creativity in the "paintings" element. Just ensure you don't trade the word order of the important thing-phrase phrases. Use the appropriate phrases you located for your research.

•If you can't use the primary key-phrase or key-word word in your studies listing, go with the drift directly to the following. Your name wishes to make feel, so use properly English grammar, and absolutely kingdom the problem you are solving. Don't stuff the call and subtitle with plenty of keywords questioning that this can assist you promote greater books. You best need some authentic key phrases in each pick out out to be determined and function people purchase your ebook. Titles and subtitles with lots of key terms are a flip off to most customers.

Hack 6 is finished. Now you've got were given a compass so as to guide the course of the rest of your e-book. As you drift through the Hacks, you will need to tweak the decision, subtitle, or series call. No troubles. Go earlier and trade them, but use the same movement elements above to extend the new get admission to.

Chapter 4: How To Make A Book Mindmap

Hack 7 receives the whole thing you recognize about your issue count number (or at the least most of what you apprehend) from your mind and onto paper. The manner to do that is to boom a Mindmap. If you are unusual with Mindmaps, go to Lifehacker.Com for extra records. A Mindmap is like gathering materials to construct the foundation of your property.

The writing technique we begin in Hack 7 will help you avoid writer's block. You will constantly understand what you need to write down and why it is essential. You won't overlook topics and want to feature them later. Your writing is probably prepared and feature go along with the waft – a few thing prized via non-fiction readers and a few other extraordinary purpose for them to buy future books from you.

Here are the motion steps for Hack 7: How to Make a Book Mindmap

•Print out copies of the word processing and spreadsheet files you created inside the preceding steps.

•Get a massive sheet of paper in case you don't have one. Collect numerous pens or pencils for whilst you're jotting notes.

•Read via your word processing and spreadsheet files to refresh your memory. I endorse going via them severa instances each.

•Write your micro-challenge matter and answer inside the middle of the net page and draw a circle round it.

•Create a Mindmap with the whole lot you don't forget is essential to your readers to apprehend about your difficulty be counted. Create a Mindmap that has at least 100 particular gadgets on it. Use items for your documents and spreadsheet as activates.

Again, communicate over with the Mindmap rationalization net site if you want help on a manner to try this.

•Put a superstar beside the fifteen most critical objects at the Mindmap you created. These is probably the beginning economic catastrophe subjects for your draft define within the next step.

•Software Alert! After I increase the number one Mindmap, every so often I create an virtual version, which include more mind throughout the arrival section. I advocate XMIND to try this due to the reality the software program is simple to apply and loose.

You can use software program to create a Mindmap, however I like to start with paper and pen. In my experience, writing appears to attract more out of me than typing does.

I use pen and paper, after which I circulate the ensuing Mindmap to the laptop, making modifications and additions. This works nicely. Most Mindmap software utility allows you to copy the textual content and paste it right into a phrase processing record so no time is wasted.

If you don't convert the handwritten Mindmap to an virtual format, I advise growing a take a look at of your Mindmap and saving it to the identical folder in which your documents and spreadsheet are placed.

Check Hack 7 off the listing! I take a few days off after finishing this step. My thoughts goals a damage, and it allows my subconscious to kind out the facts and make connections. Remember, all paintings and no play make Jack a totally stupid boy! Go do something you experience.

HOW TO CREATE AN OUTLINE FAST

In Hack 8, you may create a draft outline. I will show you a manner to create an outline that allows you to be easy to do and bring notable outcomes. Please don't bypass this hack! The hassle most humans run into is that they have got been now not taught in college a manner to create an define that works. In this hack, I will display you a way to create one on the way to help your writing and not kill you at the same time.

A correct outline is the most crucial part of fast writing. Writer's block most often stems now not from a lack of motivation, but from a lack of path. A appropriate outline paves the street in your writing and publishing achievement. Learn a manner to do that and developing books will become less difficult and lots less painful. This has been proper for me and I choice is probably for you.

One exceptional detail earlier than we start. The next steps will ask you to apply each the innovative right side of your brain and the more logical left element. Most authors warfare in their writing because they're trying to be inventive and logical in tandem. This blocks properly writing and leave the author staring at a few sentences at the pc display show screen. Let me inspire you as strongly as I can to use each your inspired issue or logical side, however no longer every on the same time.

Hack 8 is a proper-mind hack. As you go through this step, make certain to apply as a fantastic deal creativity as you may. Here are the movement elements for Hack eight: Creating a Fast Outline:

•Gather the files, spreadsheets, and the Mindmap you created and function them to be had. Use the data on them at any point in this hack.

•Write a listing of the fifteen maximum important mind you starred on your Mindmap. Work thru the list and pass off 5 of the devices. The ultimate ten are the subjects for each of your e-book chapters.

•Take 5 sheets of paper and write one of the ten topics on the pinnacle of each facet.

•Now, write twelve questions underneath each topic. The questions need to be ones you accept as true with your reader is asking you. Do this by means of way of using asking "who" questions, "what" questions, "why" questions, "wherein" questions, "while" questions, and two "how" questions. It allows me to count on in reality one among my readers is sitting with me in a espresso shop and we're chatting. I write the questions he or she asks me about my situation rely within the route of our imaginary go to. This might sound loopy, but howdy, we are on the creative aspect of the thoughts right now!

•Under each problem matter, select out the 9 questions you take into account are the most important on your reader and do away with the relaxation from the list.

•Book Alert! If you need extra records on writing speedy, I propose finding out WRITING FAST by way of using the use of Jeff Bollow. I tailor-made and modified severa of his mind to create a extraordinary quicker writing approach.

Congratulations! You completed Hack 8 and created a FAST OUTLINE that presentations the questions and troubles that scenario your readers in recent times. Your ebook might be greater useful and reader-targeted. Readers will sit up straight for brand spanking new e-book releases from you due to the reality they recognize you've got were given their quality interests in thoughts.

Chapter 5: How To Develop A Focused Outline

We flow into to the logical aspect of the thoughts for Hack nine. You will take the FAST OUTLINE you created in Hack 8 and fill it in with vital statistics. These will characteristic writing turns on and research elements within the next hacks. Use the substances you already advanced for this ebook (your documents, spreadsheet, and Mindmap) to offer the define greater specifics.

A FOCUSED OUTLINE assures your ebook covers the maximum critical records, flows without troubles, and connects with the reader. This tool will help you write and finish your manuscript a good deal quicker than conventional techniques. Another advantage of this method is it releases your complete creativity, on the same time as writing the FAST DRAFT. You can be amazed and thrilled with the thoughts that come to you inside the next step due to the reality you organized your self on this hack.

Here are the movement factors for Hack nine: Developing a Focused Outline

•Gather the files, spreadsheets, and the Mindmap you created and function them available. Use the statistics on them at any point on this hack.

•Create a present day phrase processing file the use of the format "Your Book Title – [Month] [Year]." Change the Month and Year as suitable.

•Type the ten financial disaster subjects in the file and trade to the Heading 1 fashion.

•Type the nine questions for every bankruptcy topic and make certain they'll be the usage of the Normal style.

•Rearrange the questions for each bankruptcy trouble be counted in a logical order. Depending on your challenge depend variety, set up the questions step-by using-step, in chronological order, or grouped into three subsections.

•Continue to apply the Normal style putting for the subsequent 3 steps.

•Go to the number one question and ask yourself what the maximum important trouble you need to mention as a way to answer the reader's question. Write that as a quick word and writing spark off.

•Then, ask yourself what the second maximum vital element you need to say to answer the reader. Write your answer as some different quick phrase and writing prompt.

•Ask yourself final factors you need to percent together along with your reader. Write every of those answers as a quick word and writing set off.

•Repeat the previous movement objects till you create four short terms/writing activates underneath each question in every financial ruin subject bear in mind.

You may be tempted to assume Hack nine takes an excessive amount of time and you need no longer be this precise. The time you spend on Hack 9 will reduce your research and writing time in half of. That's right, I stated in half!

While it'd feel silly, do the paintings. You can count on thru each part of your e-book now, or you may do it later. The truth is you will should do the artwork, so truly do that hack now. Doing the "thinking through the e-book" detail at the identical time as you are studying or writing assures you could get sidetracked and do more paintings that in no way makes it into your ebook.

Finished with the hack? Well accomplished! Let's maintain the ball rolling and go with the flow immediately to Hack 10 – How to Write a Fast Draft

HOW TO WRITE A FAST DRAFT

We bypass decrease once more to the right issue of the mind with Hack 10. In this hack, you take the unique outline you advanced in the very last hack and use it to amplify your FAST DRAFT. But we're in a function to name it your rapid draft due to the truth the aim is to put in writing it as rapid as you can so that you can permit the modern part of your thoughts run wild.

The hacks up to date have positioned a remarkable deal of records internal of you. Your unconscious has been making connections, and you may have stuck yourself wondering over the e-book even as you were away from your table. You probable have idea of latest and exciting thoughts. This hack permits you get them on paper so you can mould and shape them in later hacks.

A key tool on this hack is the "Idea Bin." After I observe Jeff Bollow's book, "Writing Fast," I used an Idea Bin and located it very beneficial. The concept of an "Idea Bin" is having an area to position new mind and mind that stand up as you are writing rapid. Instead of chasing the rabbit whilst you are writing, make a be aware about it inside the Idea Bin, and use it inside the subsequent Hack.

Here are the motion points for Hack 10: How to Write a Fast Draft:

•Open the Focused Outline you created in the last hack. Type the name and subtitle of your e-book on the pinnacle of the number one page and use the end up aware of and subtitle styles to exchange their font.

•Open some different word processing document and preserve it as "Idea Bin – [Month] [Year]" changing Month and Year as appropriate.

•Set a timer for 25 minutes.

•Start with the number one bankruptcy and write four- to five-sentence paragraphs for each writing set off. Work on the first bankruptcy by myself at some point of these 25 mins. Don't skip right now to the subsequent economic ruin if you finish early.

•Do now not write introductions or conclusions in the in the meantime. You will try this in a later hack. Your goal on this hack is to put in writing down the "meat" of your ebook as short as feasible.

•If a new concept takes area to you as you're writing the fast draft, record it inside the Idea Bin and cross lower back to typing the chapter at once. Don't correct your grammar, spelling, or style. Try to put in writing as speedy as you can. You will clean up the manuscript in a later hack. Just have a laugh and don't worry. Be glad! Mistakes don't do not forget.

•If you quote from a e book or an writer but can't remember the selection or come to be aware of, virtually placed a few element like "the writing e-book that has the inexperienced cover" or a few detail comparable. No rely what, don't forestall the drift. You will fill inside the ones records later.

•When the timer is going off, forestall writing. Get up out of your writing table and take a damage for five minutes. Do a few element that requires bodily movement. Take a stroll. Wash the dishes. Exercise. Do yoga.

•After 5 to ten minutes, pass lower lower back in your writing desk and repeat the previous 5 steps for the subsequent financial disaster. If you didn't cease the monetary spoil you have got been operating on over the past consultation, maintain to put in writing that financial destroy. Always paintings on one financial ruin at a time. If you finish a financial catastrophe early. Take a break early. Don't skip right now to the following economic spoil.

•Repeat the ones movement elements until you write a FAST DRAFT of the 10 chapters on your ebook. Depending in your time desk, you could want to alter the harm times among writing segments.

And that's Hack 10. You aim in this hack changed into to use the writing factors to create four- to five-sentence paragraphs and create your FAST DRAFT. You now have a FAST DRAFT that connects with the reader and to which it will likely be clean to function even greater price.

As you have been writing and putting ideas inside the Idea Bin, you determined regions that desired more data or have been inclined in content material. We will cover how to research and fill in those gaps within the subsequent hack.

HOW TO DO QUALITY RESEARCH FOR YOUR BOOK

Congratulations! You are midway through writing your ebook. Welcome to Hack eleven: How to Do Quality Research for Your Book.

You can be amazed that I haven't requested you to do any e-book studies till this element. The purpose is straightforward – maximum authors do loads of research that in no way grow to be in their e book because of this they spend time doing e book studies that is not wanted. I don't want you to make the identical mistake.

Other authors do a bargain of research, piece together what others have stated, and end up with a e-book that lacks passion and an high-quality glide. It gives the have an effect on that a machine in preference to a person wrote the e-book. Readers don't revel in the ones sorts of books as hundreds, and you want your reader to revel in your ebook!

Research is crucial; don't get me wrong. The cause of research is to reinforce your ebook and provide your reader the exceptional information feasible. The key to genuine research is a robust facts of what you're looking for along aspect your efforts. I will display you the way to try this in this hack.

Here are the movement factors for Hack 11: How to Do Quality Research for Your Book

•Print out your FAST DRAFT and feature a study the complete manuscript in a single sitting.

•Read through your FAST DRAFT again marking paragraphs in the following manner:

•Put a superstar beside any paragraph that desires a reference — an writer, a e-book, a internet internet page, and many others.

•Draw a rectangular beside any paragraph that goals more statistics — a quote, more element, an photograph, and so forth.

•Place a circle beside any paragraph that wishes to be extra focused — a better concept, a listing of steps, a stronger description, and many others.

•Open your FAST DRAFT report and workout styles to the paragraphs you marked in the following way:

•Heading three: Highlight the paragraphs you placed a movie star beside and study the "Heading three" style.

•Heading 4: Highlight the paragraphs you marked with a square and exercise the "Heading 4" fashion.

•Heading five: Highlight the paragraphs you marked with a circle and take a look at the "Heading 5" fashion.

•Use your Idea Bin to bolster sections or paragraphs. Then, paintings via the paragraphs for your manuscript and upload studies from the Internet, books, interviews, and so forth. Type the records at the surrender of the paragraph.

•Don't fear approximately running your Idea Bin mind and studies into the manuscript proper now. We do this inside the next hack. Your purpose with this hack is to locate the studies and positioned it beside the paragraph that desires it. Your research will circulate an lousy lot extra fast in case you don't write and research at the identical time.

How did this approach provide you with the consequences you need? Wasn't it incredible to bolster your ebook with studies that mattered? Aren't you satisfied you didn't spend limitless hours in research that ended up inside the trash? I am eager on this hack due to the fact I don't waste time, and it improves my ebook too!

Take time to perform a little aspect you revel in. Reward your self for paintings well performed. You have completed the heavy lifting factors of writing a ebook and the rest of the hacks will fall into area. We're seeing slight at the surrender of the tunnel!

HOW TO DEVELOP A FOCUSED DRAFT

Hack 12 will assist you're taking your research and FAST DRAFT and blend them right right into a FOCUSED DRAFT. The FAST DRAFT have become a innovative "right mind" hack. The FOCUSED DRAFT is a logical "left thoughts" hack. Your FAST DRAFT has lots of mind and mind, but they aren't as focused and compelling as they want to be. Hack 12 will help you recognition the manuscript and make it much less tough on your reader to understand.

Here are the movement points for Hack 12: How to Develop a Focused Draft.

•Gather the documents, spreadsheets, and the Mindmap you created and characteristic them available. Don't forget about approximately to use statistics from them at any factor in this hack.

•Open your ebook report and pick out out "Find" in the Home toolbar. This will convey up a navigation panel in which you may pick out "Headings" and flow a few of the incredible Headings. Right click on on on the panel and pick out out "Choose Heading Level," then pick out out Heading 3.

•Heading three paragraphs need a reference – an author, a e-book, a internet web page, and so forth. Work through each of these paragraphs for your record to weave the actual paragraph and your research together. The give up cease result may be an extended paragraph. Sometimes, you may need to create paragraphs. When you finish weaving the facts together, highlight the paragraph(s) and exchange the fashion from Heading three to Normal.

•Right click on at the navigation panel, select "Choose Heading Level," and pick out Heading 4.

•Heading 4 paragraphs need greater facts – a quote, a element, an picture, and masses of others. Work via each of these paragraphs to your report to weave the unique paragraph and your research collectively. Heading four paragraphs generally need to be extended. When you end weaving the facts together, spotlight the paragraph(s) and alternate the fashion from Heading 4 to Normal.

•Right click on the navigation pane, pick "Choose Heading Level," and select Heading 5.

•Heading five paragraphs want to be greater targeted – they want a higher concept, a list of steps, a more potent description, and so on. Work thru every of these paragraphs on your report to weave the specific paragraph and your research collectively. Heading 5 paragraphs often want to be prolonged too. When you finish weaving the statistics collectively, spotlight the paragraph(s) and alternate the fashion from Heading 5 to Normal.

•Now is the time to determine if the "scaffold" questions you used as writing activates should stay in your manuscript or no longer. Sometimes, leaving the questions permits the go with the flow and wonderful instances it does no longer. I'll depart that preference to you. Most of the time, I put off the questions due to the truth they served as scaffolding and the framework of the residence is now in vicinity.

And that's Hack 12: How to Develop a Focused Draft. I desire you found this hack beneficial.

Several eBook authors advise the use of Scrivener software program. Having attempted it myself, the hassle I bumped into turned into that gaining knowledge of the manner to apply the software program software emerge as time-consuming. The fundamental benefit people stated became the benefit of business organisation, but I locate Wo... masses less difficult to navigate. ... clean hack of changing paragraph p... to keep song of edits helps a incredibl... Plus, I really have used Word all the tim... I can write books and not spending t... studying a modern software progra... application software.

Completing Hack 12 method that the "meat" of your e-book is in place. Have you been surprised that we haven't worked on introductions or conclusions yet? Now is the fine time to install writing those, so permit's turn to the ones inside the next hack.

Chapter 6: How To Write Good Conclusions

How you take a look at a book and the manner you write a e-book aren't the equal. In fact, appropriate authors recognize you write a e-book backwards: first the frame, then the belief, and ultimately the Introduction. I located out this hack in my PhD seminars.

In Hack 13, we're capable of write the economic spoil conclusions first. Then, we are capable of write the belief for the entire e-book. We will great write conclusions in this hack.

You may additionally wonder why we are specializing in writing the conclusions on my own. The motive is easy. Lots of papers, articles, and books have correct content material cloth, but fall flat of their conclusions. This is sad due to the fact the conclusion is the closing difficulty the reader encounters so it wants to be first rate.

In this hack, I will show you a easy manner to install writing robust conclusions that depart the reader trying greater. "Wanting extra" at the quit of a financial catastrophe, way they'll turn the internet internet web page and take a look at the subsequent bankruptcy. "Wanting more" on the stop of the e-book, way they'll need to shop for your next e book due to the reality they understand you supply the goods.

So, permit's do Hack thirteen: How to Write Good Conclusions

•Open your FOCUSED DRAFT phrase processing file.

•Go to the primary chapter.

•At the give up of the bankruptcy, write four paragraphs (every paragraph need to embody three to 5 sentences):

•What the reader located on this financial destroy

•Why they must placed this bankruptcy into exercise

•Encouragement to apply the financial disaster

•How we are transitioning from this bankruptcy to the following one

•Repeat the previous movement steps for each chapter.

•Go to the stop of your report and create a new Heading 1 called "Conclusion."

•In the Conclusion section, create three subsections and layout them with Heading 2: "Why It Is Important," "What You Have Learned," and "You Can Do This!"

•Copy and paste every of the number one paragraphs in the economic break conclusions to the "What You Have Learned" subsection inside the order they get up to your ebook.

•Copy and paste each of the second one paragraphs within the chapter conclusions to "Why It Is Important" subsection in the order they seem for your e-book.

•Copy and paste each of the 1/three paragraphs within the chapter conclusions to "You Can Do This!" subsection inside the order they appear on your e-book.

•In the "Why It Is Important" subsection, use the cloth you copied and pasted to create a precis of the significance of this subject matter and reaffirm the reader's preference to observe. Delete cloth you don't use.

•In the "What You Have Learned" subsection, use the cloth you copied and pasted to create a precis of the crucial gadgets the reader found for your e book. Use a listing of bullet factors to move over the principle thoughts. Delete fabric you don't use.

•In the "You Can Do This!" subsection, use the material you copied and pasted to create a motivational "speech" to encourage your reader to get commenced out in recent times. Thank them for analyzing your e-book and ask them to deliver you remarks so you could make upgrades for destiny readers. Again, delete material you don't use.

•Decide in case you want to apply the Heading 2 headings or delete them.

This hack indicates you a way to put in writing down conclusions that hook up with each unique and purpose a robust give up on your complete ebook.

If you are like me, you have got have been given examine many books that lose steam at the quit. Using this hack ensures that this received't take place to your ebook.

I used to marvel what to say in a quit, however not anymore. The 4 paragraphs provide you with a template that meets the desires of your reader. You might be thrilled how effects your conclusions go with the flow after analyzing this hack.

Continuing in "backwards order," we circulate from writing conclusions to writing the introductions within the next Hack.

HOW TO WRITE INTERESTING INTRODUCTIONS

Many authors write at a snail's tempo because of the reality they write their creation first. High-manufacturing authors recognize to write down the introduction very last! If you try to write the advent first, you'll discover you don't have sufficient statistics to make it actual. Often, a easy net page is the exceptional give up end result.

I desire I had located out this in advance than I worked on my PhD software program, as my papers and primary ebook would possibly had been a fantastic deal stronger. Surely some thing so essential to writing could have been protected in one of the English instructions I attended? Unfortunately now not. Go determine!

In Hack 14: How to Write Interesting Introductions, I will provide you with each other smooth template to help you create first-rate introductions. You will discover ways to write the Introduction for the entire e book. You will see that ready until this component in the hacks to put in writing the introductions makes them smooth as compared on your preceding experience.

So, permit's get busy with Hack 14: How to Write Interesting Introductions:

•Open your FOCUSED DRAFT on your phrase processing record.

•Go to the primary chapter.

•At the begin of the financial catastrophe write at the least paragraphs:

•The Attention Paragraph(s)

•This paragraph have to take hold of the reader's hobby approximately the hassle covered in the bankruptcy.

•Examples encompass mentioning an event from information, telling a personal story, announcing a few trouble that might marvel the reader, quoting a well-known man or woman, or some element else to get the reader's hobby.

•The Direction Paragraph(s)

•This paragraph must detail the course the bankruptcy will take to cowl the state of affairs.

•Examples encompass a thesis announcement, list your step-with the useful resource of-step technique, listing subtopics in order and describing the warfare so one can be resolved.

•Repeat the previous motion steps for each bankruptcy.

•Now, visit the start of your file, create a cutting-edge heading referred to as "Introduction," and format it with the Heading 1 fashion.

•In the Introduction section, create four subsections and format them with Heading 2: "What this Book is About," "My Story," "Who This Book is For," and "What We Will Accomplish."

•Clearly gift the problem the ebook goes to resolve in the "What This Book is About" subsection. Include observations of the manner humans have tried to clear up this trouble. Empathize with certainly each person jogging thru this form of trouble. This subsection have to be numerous paragraphs long.

•In the "My Story" subsection, write numerous paragraphs about how you struggled with the trouble of the ebook and the way you discovered the answer you will be sharing. Share your qualifications to install writing the ebook. The fact you have an answer gives you credibility. Let your reader recognize you address them and want to help. People don't care about what you apprehend until they apprehend which you care.

•Many functionality readers will pick "Read Inside" desire to preview your ebook first to decide inside the event that they want to buy it. Writing the subsection known as "Who This Book is For" will help them make that desire. It will weed out ability terrible evaluations at the same time as you u . S . Your target market. I typically have bullet lists because the number one part of this subsection: one which describes my target marketplace and a few different that describes readers who will no longer gain from my ebook.

•Copy and paste each of the "Direction" paragraphs inside the financial disaster introductions to the "What We Will Accomplish" subsection inside the order they seem on your ebook.

•In the "What We Will Accomplish" subsection, use the fabric you copied and pasted to create a summary of the crucial gadgets the reader will have a look at on your ebook. Use a bullet list to summarize the primary points.

•After you write each of the sections, retitle them to suggest the form of e-book you have written. Most of the time, I drop the "What This Book is About" subsection

Heading and that subsection serves because the "introduction" paragraph of the Introduction Section.

And that's Hack 14: How to Write Interesting Introductions.

You positioned out the manner to jot down down brief bankruptcy introductions that capture the reader's hobby and put together them for the primary factors within the financial ruin. Then, you found out a manner to create an thrilling ebook introduction that devices the degree for the reader to keep turning pages.

Good introductions height curiosity. Using the e-book advent template in this hack will boom your e-book profits. The truth that your e-book accomplishes what it devices out to do will bring about more evaluations. Reviews are tough to get, so some component you can do to assistance is precious!

You can also furthermore were writing introductions in advance than we were given to Hack 14. That's no hassle. I encourage you to check your preceding artwork and decorate it with those creation hacks.

Now you've got got were given written the frame of the e-book, the conclusions, and the introductions. Are there any duties left to do? Yes, we want to paintings thru one extra hack earlier than the report is ready for editing. Let's comb via you ebook one greater time and make it stronger.

HOW TO MAKE A FINAL DRAFT STRONG

I don't recognise approximately you, however books with obvious errors are a actual turn off to me. I've spent my hard-earned money and trusted the writer to supply an high-quality product. Mistakes are the sign of shoddy workmanship. Maybe the individual that wrote the ebook emerge as clearly seeking to make a brief greenback. I fantastic received't purchase from him or her yet again!

Writing a e-book is an extended adventure (as you well recognise). Part of the motive errors creep into a e-book is that the author loses steam on the stop line and sincerely desires to get the e-book available. I've skilled that feeling with each e-book I've written. You hit a wall. Without caution, spelling, grammar, formatting, and price begin to become a lot tons much less critical.

That's why you want Hack 15. Follow the steps on this hack to ensure you supply your reader a scrumptious meal and no longer leave an lousy taste in their mouth!

So, allow's get cooking with Hack 15: How to Strengthen a Final Draft

•Open your FOCUSED DRAFT report

•Content

•For each bankruptcy, consider a non-public example out of your life or someone famous that illustrates what you are explaining in the financial ruin. Weave that story into the monetary destroy inside the region that makes the maximum revel in.

•For each financial ruin, studies a quote from a famous person on that challenge depend. Insert the quote and author at the front of the economic ruin. Format the quote and writer using the QUOTE STYLE, if you are the usage of Microsoft Word. If you are the use of every different word processing software program, choose its fashion for expenses.

•For each financial catastrophe, insert a high-quality useful useful aid the reader can use. Potential assets encompass internet web websites, software program, or an eBook written with the aid of the usage of way of every other writer. Don't reference each specific e-book you have got were given published, as you will do that on the give up of the e book.

•Grammar and Spelling

•Run the spelling and grammar checker. Make extraordinary your phrase processing software program is prepared to test each spelling and grammar in File-Options-Proofing.

•Search for "There is" and rewrite every highlighted sentence with an active verb.

•Remove the terms "very" and "simply" except the sentence makes no sense with out them.

•Search and Replace (in Word). Use the following facts to do away with greater paragraph marks and line carriages on your record. You should no longer have regions amongst sentences or areas that appear between durations and Word's paragraph marks.

•Search ^l (little L) and update with ^p (update all)

•Search for ^p<region>^p and replace with ^p (update all)

•Search for ^p^p and replace with ^p (replace all)

•Search for < areas> and replace with <one space> (update all)

•Search for <period><area>^p and replace with <length>^p (update all)

•Keywords

•Review the listing of key terms you superior in Hack five.

•Work through every name of your chapters and be aware if you could rewrite the call the usage of one in each of your key phrases or key-word terms.

•Work thru every section name (in case you prepared your book that manner) and repeat the previous action thing.

•Save your record as FINAL DRAFT.

The steps you took in Hack 15 have taken your ebook to a ultra-modern stage. You brought extra price and made the e-book less tough to study and layout. You corrected a number of your grammar and spelling mistakes, making the e-book go with the flow higher.

Without Hack 15, your e-book might resemble many books sold on Kindle: whole of mistakes. Reviewers are quick to component this out to potential shoppers. You don't want that to arise.

At this component in writing a e-book, I see the stop line, however experience exhausted. Sometimes quitting looks like an wonderful choice. But it isn't. I need to inspire you to complete the race. Keep your self brought about and preserve going. You are almost there!

Now we've a nicely-prepared ebook that addresses a hassle the reader cares about with a strong answer. The e-book is thrilling, empathetic, and written well. It flows from one economic spoil to the following and is easy to study.

We have one more hack to do with the manuscript. We want to shine your phrases in order that they shine! We cover that hack next.

Chapter 7: How To Polish The Finished Manuscript

In Hack sixteen, I will display you the manner to get your book professionally proofread and formatted for a superb deal a great deal much less cash than you would possibly count on. If you are like me, having a few other person correct your ebook can be hard. You spent lots of effort and time to deliver something from now not a few thing. Sometimes it honestly seems incorrect that a few other person ought to get the venture of declaring the subjects that want to be superior.

Maybe we want to think about this a awesome manner. Imagine that you had designed and built the conventional '65 Ford Mustang Hardtop: an unsurpassed feat of engineering and design. Unfortunately, as you were constructing the car, a few elements were given grimy, and a skinny layer of dust settled over the automobile. It's nevertheless an wonderful automobile, honestly no longer as awesome as it could be. You employed a professional to return wash your car and follow a excessive gloss coat of wax. Wow! Now the auto is a masterpiece.

Hiring a professional to perform the splendor of your Mustang is similar to hiring specialists to proofread and layout your ebook for Kindle. They add price to some thing that is already excellent.

I need to reveal you the way to hire professionals who will do an first rate undertaking and no longer charge an outrageous rate.

Here are the motion steps for Hack 16: How to Polish the Final Draft

Finding a Proofreader:

•Go to www.Elance.Com and positioned up a project for a proofreader. You need to encompass the priority, name, and subtitle of your e-book. Include the range of phrases for your manuscript. Accept proposals for seven days and set the fee as "Under $500."

•When you submit the concept, Elance.Com will advise freelancers to invite in your advertised function. Don't take delivery of the freelancers that Elance.Com shows. Instead, visit the search bar, pick "Freelancers," type "proofreader" in the bar, and pick out "Go."

•Sort the results via the subsequent criteria on the left panel: "At Least five large call Feedback" and "At Least 15 Reviews." This will slim the results a awesome deal. Right click at the number one twenty people in the are seeking list and choose out "Open in New Tab." Look at their portfolio. If their customer repeat price is thirty percentage or better, pick out the "Hire Me" button. You obtained't be hiring them at this factor, but sending them a request to make a suggestion for your proofreading hobby.

•Repeat the preceding step till you have got have been given despatched requests for a bid to thirty human beings. You might also kind through 50 to 60 people in the list to reap this end end result.

•Freelancers on Elance.Com will ship you bids to your venture. "Hide" any that don't meet your requirements. "Hide" any which can be too pricey or too cheap. Narrow the arena to 10 vendors. Send every of those humans a short email asking how they display the modifications they may make for your record if you pick out them.

•Choose the provider who replies on your e-mail right away and has an offer based totally on half a cent regular with word to do your proofreading. Award them the vicinity and follow the Elance.Com suggestions to control the job.

•After you get the book lower again from the proofreader, check the adjustments they made, ask them to do any crucial comply with-up art work, and rename the report "BOOK FINAL – SEND TO DESIGNER".

Finding a Kindle Format Designer

•Follow the identical method for finding a proofreader on Elance.Com unique above and you may discover a Kindle Book Format Designer.

•Don't send the finalist an electronic mail asking how they show adjustments they've got made for your report. Instead, ask your finalist to supply you PDFs of Kindle books they have designed that could artwork for your type of ebook.

•A appropriate Kindle Format Designer expenses greater or less much like a proofreader.

•Send them the file "BOOK FINAL – SEND TO DESIGNER" and ask them to supply you once more a report organized to be uploaded to Kindle. When you obtain the file, test it with the Kindle Preview software application to be had on the Kindle internet page. If everything appears real, approve the Elance.Com assignment and pay the freelancer. If the preview has troubles, contact the freelancer to make corrections and then cease the task.

Hack 16 sent the e-book to other experts so they might do their magic. I confirmed you how to find out a splendid proofreader and Kindle Interior Book Designer. You can use this hack each time you want to outsource part of your publishing empire.

A huge mistake I made come to be seeking to do the proofreading and formatting myself. Writing books is my expertise; proofreading and formatting are not. As a end end result, I wasted too much time learning the way to professionally proofread and layout Kindle books once I need to have spent that point writing greater books. The key to fulfillment at the Kindle platform is producing greater books.

If you comply with the hacks on this ebook, you may write a ebook that people want to shop for. You will recoup your funding. I can't promise the ones subjects, of path. You are mastering the hacks which have taken my books from selling a few every week to selling numerous an afternoon. That's why I am confident you could do the identical detail.

Don't sabotage your efforts by the use of freeing a e-book packed with errors or one that is hard to observe because of horrible formatting. You don't want the reader to drop out of the reading experience mulling over your spelling, grammar, or the ebook's terrible formatting. As quickly as they do, they've dropped out of the "experience" of your e-book and the chances of them becoming repeat clients has been misplaced.

You don't want readers to observe your interior ebook format, however you do want them to love your cover. We'll walk thru a way to layout a excellent eBook cover within the subsequent hack.

WHERE TO GET GOOD BOOK COVER IDEAS

I need people didn't judge books with the useful aid in their covers, however they do. Let me percentage a private tale. I employed a photograph artist to layout my first ebook cover with hundreds of my feedback. When we finished the project, I uploaded the cover to the Kindle platform and waited for a flood of e book profits. I simply knew it have grow to be going to be a rainmaker. But we noticed a drop of rain each few days.

Back in the ones days, if you had checked out my ebook cowl in assessment to the others in my beauty, you can have determined that it stood out. It didn't resemble any of the alternative covers. At first, I concept this come to be a extremely good aspect. After a while, I determined out this changed into a very terrible aspect.

People expect books in every style to appear to be every different. My book screamed "novice!" as it didn't healthful the fashion.

In Hack 17, I will display you how to discover your fashion's coloration pallet and design limits. Use this statistics to region your e-book squarely within the fashion and prepared to compete, regardless of the huge publishers. In reality, you could piggyback on marketplace studies they have got carried out and not spend a penny.

Here are the motion steps for Hack 17: Where to Get Good Book Cover Ideas

•Go to Amazon.Com. Make fantastic you are not signed into your Amazon account because of the truth this can trade the consequences based totally totally on books you obtain in the past.

•Choose KINDLE STORE from the menu.

•Enter [Your Book Topic] within the are trying to find bar and pick GO. The are trying to find effects embody the top promoting books within the Kindle shop in your style – your opposition.

•Choose "Image View." This will change the hunt outcomes to large photographs of the e book covers.

•Create a spreadsheet with the subsequent columns: "Book Title", "Book Title Color", "Color #1", "Color #2", "Color #three" and "Design."

•Start with the number one e-book and fill inside the spreadsheet columns.

•Most ebook covers use three hues. Designers use colour #1 the most, coloration #2 2nd maximum, and shade #three for highlights.

•Most e-book covers in a style will percentage a similar subject matter.

Describe the picture or layout used inside the cover within the "Design" column.

•Repeat the preceding step for the primary twenty books inside the search effects. If a cover is glaringly self-designed, do now not include it to your results.

•When you've got got recorded twenty entries, type the listing with the resource of the usage of shade #1. Determine the shade used the maximum. This is the precept colour you have to use on your cover.

•Sort the listing with the aid of shade #2. Look for the shade that is used the most. You ought to use this secondary shade in your cover.

•Sort the list with the beneficial useful resource of shade #three. Look for the colour used the most. Use that color as your spotlight color.

•Read the entries in the layout column. Look for the "fashion difficulty" or "fashion format."

•Write a list that consists of colour #1, color #2, shade #three, and the "fashion subject be counted."

Hack 17 locations your cowl in your e-book's fashion and ready to compete with the opportunity titles already in the marketplace.

People count on a ebook to appearance just like other books inside the style. If a e-book doesn't look the identical, readers bear in mind it is substandard. They won't be able to articulate why they suppose this manner when they check the cover, but they may skip over the ebook despite the fact that. You want to make certain your coloration scheme and layout are actually set for your e-book's fashion.

This hack doesn't take prolonged. In fact, it could be the very nice hack in this e-book.

For ebook earnings, even though, Hack 17 is the maximum important. If you have got posted books on Kindle in advance than, use this hack to remodel your cover and get better effects.

We have your ebook cowl coloration and layout concept, now permit's bypass on to the subsequent hack and discover ways to create a pleasant ebook cover.

HOW TO CREATE A QUALITY BOOK COVER

When you in all likelihood did your in advance studies on e-book covers, you truly noticed numerous unsightly covers on your style. That's properly information! If books with ugly covers are promoting, then books with appealing covers will make a killing on Kindle. This hack will assist you keep away from finishing up with an ugly cover.

The key to a lovable ebook cowl is locating a excellent fashion designer and paying for their service. Unless you are a photo fashion dressmaker, don't attempt to boom a cowl yourself.

But even in case you are a photo fashion designer, I wouldn't layout your non-public cover. Why? Because you have got out of place the objectivity had to create a bestselling ebook cowl.

We pass all over again to Elance.Com with Hack 18: How to Create a Quality Book Cover. If you put money into now not anything else, please spend it for your cover. Ignore my advice at your peril!

Here are the movement steps for Hack 18: How to Create a Quality Book Cover:

•The first rule of creating a quality ebook cover is don't do it your self. Period. Unless you apprehend what you're doing, go away this step to a e-book cowl fashion fashion designer.

•Many eBooks recommend using www.Fiverr.Com due to the fact the deliver for purchasing a exceptional book cowl. You can skip that direction, however my revel in has been you get a traditional cowl that seems like many one-of-a-type covers. If you want to get a cover completed inexpensively, but, you may use this approach.

Finding a Great Book Cover Designer

•Go to www.Elance.Com and publish a assignment for a ebook cowl format. Include the topic, name, and subtitle of your ebook in the notion. Include display display display screen pics of four or five brilliant ebook covers to your e-book's style (on your opinion). Accept proposals for seven days and set the fee as "Under $500."

•When you located up the idea, Elance.Com will advise freelancers you need to invite to use for the vicinity. Don't take transport of the freelancers that Elance.Com indicates. Instead, visit the quest bar, pick out

"Freelancers," enter "e-book cover" in the bar, and pick "Go."

•Sort the results through the subsequent necessities on the left panel: "At Least 5 massive name Feedback" and "At Least 15 Reviews." This will narrow the effects drastically. Right click on the number one twenty people within the are trying to find listing and pick out "Open in New Tab." Look at their portfolio. If their client repeat price is thirty percent or better, select out the "Hire Me" button. You received't be hiring them at this point, certainly sending them a request to make a suggestion in your proofreading assignment.

•Repeat the previous step till you ship requests for a bid to thirty humans. You may additionally moreover moreover kind through 50 to 60 human beings within the listing to obtain this result.

•Freelancers on Elance.Com will send you proposals to your assignment. "Hide" any that don't meet your requirements. "Hide" any which might be too high-priced or too cheap. Narrow the area to ten vendors. Send every of these ten a quick e mail asking wherein format they will ship you the finished ebook cowl.

•Choose the company who replies in your e-mail right away and has an offer amongst $40 and $eighty. Award them the hobby and observe Elance.Com processes to govern the mission.

•Ask the cover clothier to ship you three e-book cowl ideas. When you get maintain of the first mind, pick one and paintings with the style clothier until you have got a layout that is better than your opposition. The identify want to be smooth to have a look at. You need now not include the subtitle on the cover until it's going to assist promote more books.

Hack 18: How to Create a Quality Book Cover offers you a book cowl so as to pique the reader's hobby and guarantee them professionals produced your ebook.

Readers use key terms to find books, but they decide which ebook to buy via the cover. You can once in a while get thru with proofreading errors. You in no way break out with ebook cover errors.

If you have posted your e-book inside the past, updated it with the number one seventeen Hacks of this ebook, and despite the fact that aren't promoting more books, I recommend you convert the duvet. Yesterday.

You now have a book poised to be a Kindle bestseller. In the following Hack, we are able to show you the manner to self-put up your masterpiece.

Chapter 8: How To Self-Publish Your Book

First, I want to congratulate you on sporting out some thing few humans do on this life. You have created a e book and that may be a momentous accomplishment. You need to be satisfied with yourself. You within the mean time are an creator in each feel of the phrase.

In this hack, I will show you the stairs to put up your ebook on the Amazon Kindle platform. The Kindle platform is the biggest virtual e-book creator within the international. No one else comes even near. Amazon is privy to how to help you sell your books. If you followed the hacks on this ebook, you're equipped to feature your ebook and let Amazon sell your e book on their internet site on-line.

So, permit's get posted! Here are the motion steps for Hack 19: How to Self-Publish Your Book.

•If you don't have an Amazon account, go to www.Amazon.Com and sign up for a free account.

•If you don't have a Kindle publishing account, go to https://kdp.Amazon.Com/ and join up for a free account. You will sign up together with your Amazon account records.

•Choose the "Add New Title" orange button.

•Enter your e-book records the usage of the facts from preceding hacks.

•Check the container "This Book is Part of a Series" and fill within the key-word series information.

•Be certain to enter the seven most crucial key phrases from your key-phrase research.

•Upload your ebook cowl document.

•Upload your ebook interior document.

•Choose the "Save and Continue" orange button.

•On the subsequent page, pick out out "Worldwide rights – all territories."

•Set your e-book fee to 35% royalty and $0.Ninety 9. After weeks, exchange this to 70% royalty and lift your e-book rate to $2.Ninety nine.

•Accept the fees for distinct nations that Amazon generates.

•Check "This perceive is enrolled in Kindle Matchbook" and choose out "Free."

•Check "Allow lending for this e-book."

•Check "By clicking Save and Publish underneath..." after which choose out the "Save and Publish" orange button.

•Congratulations! You within the in the meantime are a published creator.

Your difficult artwork culminates in publishing a Kindle eBook in Hack 19: How to Self-Publish Your Book. You may be assured that your ebook meets a real need, is simple to discover, and has a cover in an effort to encourage readers to buy your ebook.

Electronic publishing presently surpasses print publishing in fashion of books provided. You observed out a skills in this e-book as a way to offer you with healthy residual earnings for future years.

You can be tempted to endure in thoughts different avenues of virtual e-book publishing outdoor of Amazon. I discourage this technique. Get the whole lot great on Amazon before thinking about specific avenues.

Amazon Kindle is the digital e-book-publishing large. You want your e-book determined on Amazon, Google, and Bing (in that order). Using a few other website in truth ensures poorer reaction than what you may enjoy on Amazon. You've worked too hard to get this factor. Don't make a mistake right here and go with every specific writer.

Now which you are a posted writer, you need to finish two extra hacks to help e book income. In the subsequent hack, we'll provide an reason behind a manner to make your e-book stand out from special books on your style on Amazon.

HOW TO MAKE YOUR BOOK STAND OUT ON AMAZON

Let's do not forget how humans purchase books on Amazon for a 2nd. Typically, they input key phrases on their issue depend of hobby inside the are looking for bar. Then, they have got a check the books that appear from their search. If they see a ebook with a pick out and cover that hobbies them, they click on on on it and visit the e-book's net internet web page.

What do capacity clients do next? They study the define of the ebook. Then, they study the writer's biography to decide if the writer is sincere. If the ebook description and author biography are awesome, they buy the ebook. If they're not, they cross again to the search listing to look for some other.

In other phrases, the define and biography most often near the sale.

In this Hack, we use a advertising and marketing and advertising reproduction acrostic that has been spherical a long term: A.I.D.A. First, we get the patron's interest. Second, we peak their hobby. Third, we create a choice to buy. Then, we supply them a particular movement step.

You can write effective advertising and marketing substances the usage of this acrostic. You can't be with the reader in person to provide an reason for the way your e-book need to assist them. Instead, you need to put in writing a compelling description and biography to do the technique for you.

So, allow's get busy! Here are the steps for Hack 20: How to Make Your Book Stand Out on Amazon.

•The first step in this hack is to update your Author Profile on Amazon.

•Go to https://authorcentral.Amazon.Com/ and sign on collectively collectively along with your Amazon account.

•Choose the "Author Page" tab.

•Choose "edit biography" and write a quick biographical essay which encompass:

•An hobby-grabbing headline

•A few paragraphs about interests you percent with the reader

•A listing of advantages (choice) the reader can anticipate from analyzing your books

•A paragraph that calls the reader to movement. In the Author Profile, the choice to motion is to take a look at about your published books.

•Add any pictures that display you engaged to your ebook's issue matter.

•The 2d step on this hack is to update your e-book description.

•Go to https://kdp.Amazon.Com

•Choose "Edit Book Details" beside the e-book you're updating.

•Go to the "Description" place and write a book description the usage of the following format. Include the top fifteen key terms from your key-phrase studies in the description in a manner that feels herbal.

•Write an eye catching headline.

•Write some paragraphs approximately what the reader find out maximum thrilling on your e-book.

•Create a bullet listing of the sorts of advantages (desire) the reader can count on from studying this e-book.

•Write a paragraph that calls the reader to movement. In the e-book description, the selection to movement is to choose the "Buy this Book" orange button.

•See this article about formatting Kindle Book Descriptions if you need to spice the outline up greater. Using the H2 Heading tag will make your headline appear in Amazon orange. (I am no longer affiliated with the net net web site mentioned above in any way, however located the information to be beneficial.)

•Software Update! If to procure the Better Book Tools software program noted earlier, you could use their module to create extremely good descriptions.

•Add instructions out of your category research using the "Add Categories" button.

•Choose the "Save and Continue" orange button.

•Check "By clicking Save and Publish beneath..." after which choose the "Save and Publish" orange button.

You created an creator's biography and e-book description that Amazon will use to aspect the right purchasers to your e-book in Hack 20: How to Make Your Book Stand Out on Amazon.

Most author profiles and ebook descriptions on Amazon are poorly written and unfocused. Well-formatted textual content stands out and has a exquisite impact. Using the "Amazon Orange" heading permits your description to in form the general feeling of Amazon.

Given the choice among a e-book with an first rate description and one with out an define (or poorly written one), which do you located the reader will buy? Bingo. This hack indicates you a way to create an creator biography and ebook description on the way to get effects.

You in the intervening time are ready to marketplace your e-book with self belief. The subsequent hack will show you smooth techniques to growth ebook profits.

HOW CAN I INCREASE BOOK SALES?

The suited information is you don't want to be a entire-time Internet marketer to your Amazon eBook to promote. The now not-so-suitable records is you continue to want to get the word out to attempting to find what you provide.

Books don't sell themselves. Even an notable ebook like yours acquired't promote itself. If people don't recognize your e book is to be had, they may't purchase it. Getting the phrase out about your e-book is crucial to growing e-book earnings.

Luckily, the Kindle platform offers numerous tactics you can sell your e-book for free of charge. Knowing the manner to apply the ones equipment will help you release a a success e-book. This hack will take you thru the steps to sell your e-book to masses of functionality shoppers at no cost.

Here are the steps for Hack 21: How Can I Increase Book Sales?

•Logon on to your Kindle publishing account: https://kdp.Amazon.Com/

•Enroll your e-book within the KDP Choose software program software.

•Choose "Promote and Advertise" in your e-book.

•Choose "Free Book Promotion."

•Choose the "Create a modern-day Free Book Promotion" orange button.

•Choose five days to sell your e-book, bearing in thoughts that

•The begin date have to be at least 10 days away

•The begin date must be on a Monday (more eBooks are downloaded on that day than every other)

•The first selling need to be for five days. Later promotions want to be or 3 days long

•Choose the "Save Changes" orange button.

•Choose the "Bookshelf" tab.

•Copy the ASIN amount and paste into an Excel spreadsheet. Record the decision of the ebook, begin date, and end date of the marketing. You will tune the outcomes of your promoting on this spreadsheet.

•Go to the Author Marketing Club net website. (I am no longer affiliated with this internet site in any manner) Submit your book statistics to the web websites. Schedule your merchandising to start in ten days' time, so the ones internet web sites may have hundreds of time to sell your e-book. Author Marketing Club isn't the handiest internet internet page with unfastened kindle selling hyperlinks, so look for others that fit your e-book style.

•After the advertising and marketing and advertising and marketing finishes, wait as a minimum per week to training consultation how your ebook did inside the merchandising.

•If the ebook sold well, run a few different advertising and advertising in ninety days. This time, sell the ebook on a Saturday and Sunday. After a month, promote the ebook over again on a Saturday and Sunday. After a month, promote the e book one extra time on a Saturday.

•If the e-book did now not promote properly, spend the following 90 days reviewing the hacks on this ebook and enhance your Kindle e-book. Change the name in case you need to, however simplest try this once. Change the duvet and word if that permits. Look at how many your e-book is in the search listing for every key-phrase. If your e-book ranks a good deal less than 10 for a keyword, attempt each exclusive key-word on your list and word if that improves profits.

And that's Hack 21: How Can I Increase Book Sales? The last hack on this e-book. You located out a manner to sign up for up for Kindle's free promoting tool and the way to inform plenty of capability clients about your advertising.

Even the incredible books can accumulate digital dirt with out a selling. Using this hack regularly will create normal profits on Amazon. Regular earnings on Amazon circulate you up the list of books they sell. Moving up the list of books Amazon promotes motives greater profits. I expect you get the idea.

You wrote your e-book to assist human beings. Promoting your ebook will positioned it in the fingers of those who need the help you provide. Marketing your ebook is like introducing a notable buddy to each different pal who desires his or her assist. Promote your e-book so others can gain from your reviews and expertise.

Chapter 9: Why Self-Positioned Up?

Self-publishing has become the ebook technique of desire for lots writers; within the past this direction, normally called arrogance publishing, was seen as most effective for those whose paintings became now not actual sufficient to be shared with readers. Well all that has modified; there are self-posted books available which might be far advanced to books which have been published with the resource of mainstream publishers. Readers are sincerely actively searching out writers which have formerly been denied to them.

If you have were given written a ebook and need to make it available to readers as soon as viable then self-publishing has large blessings to each the extremely-modern and set up writer. You can now post what you write - any style, any length, quick stories, sagas, opinions, instructional research, comedy or existence memories; it's miles your choice. Let readers determine if there is a likely market in your writing, if you are obsessed on your art work then you may most likely locate others who are too.

You have the choice to hold a larger percentage of the profits – if you create an e-book and distribute it your self you keep 100% of all sales, even if the usage of an internet shop to manipulate the sale and distribution of your ebook, e.G. Amazon or Smashwords, you preserve a great percent of the income from earnings.

You have control over the velocity of manual – your book may be available to readers in as low as 10 mins from hitting the Publish button. You can quite in reality placed up and begin selling your e-book these days.

You can self-publish completely free — submit your e-book as each a published and ebook for no earlier fees. This is top notch facts for those on a restrained budget as you may decide wherein to allocate your rate range or select out to undertake all responsibilities your self.

You want no precise competencies — nice fundamental word-processing and internet skills are had to format and add your art work; self-publishing services are smooth to use.

You maintain all of the publishing rights — you make a decision a way to post your e-book, wherein to make it to be had and at the same time as to position up. Keep your e-book available for so long as you want with no remaindering and no decreased royalties.

You decide the charge of your book – make sure your ebook is every priced competitively and offers you the possibility to maximise your income. Selling at a low price may boom your profits, if there's a constrained market on your art work then probable a higher charge is better.

You decide to adopt as lots or as little of the publishing, vending and earnings responsibilities as you choice - buy in offerings you experience are simply well worth searching for both to enhance your ebook or to give your self greater time to commit to your writing.

You have get right of access to to a big style of distribution options – self-publishing services provide distribution channels that encompass online retailers and excessive road bookstores. You can also promote your books in stores that could seem lots less obvious, e.G. Your close by preserve, locations of ancient interest, at your schooling and presentation sports, and to relevant interest organizations. You can also approach your close by bookshops as many are most effective too pleased to stock books through a neighborhood author.

You can make modifications to your e-book for the duration of its lifespan – change the price to beautify income, add pages to sell your new books, add new hyperlinks to applicable assets or to your website, accurate any errors found after e book, alternate the duvet, or alternate the call. At some thing you may need to adopt substantial changes or updates; all you need to do is submit a new edition.

You layout your personal promoting method – use techniques that meet your possibilities and those of your readers; blog, tweet, supply talks or readings, create a net website or use targeted marketing.

If you want to you could even sell your e-book to a traditional creator after self-publishing - shops and publishers are simply seeking to self-published books and offering contracts; on occasion this will be beneficial if you could steady an remarkable boom.

In brief you have got whole manage over your e-book.

If you have written a ebook that you need to make to be had to readers then the query is - why may want to you now not self-publish?

2 - Your self-publishing alternatives

You first want to determine which self-publishing options super suit you and your e book. Start through using asking yourself the following questions and offer you with a publishing plan that meets your desires.

Do you want to look your e-book to be had as an e-book, published ebook or both?

The quickest manner to post your e book and begin selling is to put up an e-book. Many writers located up an ebook first after which placed up a published version at a later date. Of route in case you art work as a instructor or public speaker you may properly want published copies of your e book to promote at activities.

Do you've got a price range for publishing or have you made a decision to undertake all the duties yourself?

You can also decide to undertake all publishing obligations yourself if you want to can help you put up your e-book and make it to be had to readers in each located out and e-book formats for no fee. You may additionally moreover moreover decide to shop for in offerings, the ones can include proofreading and enhancing, cowl format, and garage if you decide to charge a print run. Make a list of offerings you may determine on to shop for in after which prioritise them.

How plenty time do you want to allocate to publishing, earnings and distribution?

The actual publishing approach may be pretty short, it is able to take a great deal less than an hour, however dealing with earnings and distribution can take in huge time. Decide whether you need extra time writing and less time on management duties or choose to adopt a high-quality deal of the artwork your self. If you select to tackle profits and distribution you could need to ensure you have were given storage area for published books, have time to maintain up to date with orders and are able to create a internet web site from which readers can order your books, download your ebooks and make payments.

Where do you want your e-book to appear in the marketplace? Amazon? Your close by e-book save?

If you want to promote thru Amazon, iBookstore, Barnes and Noble and others you will find this less difficult if you submit the usage of each Amazon and Smashwords.

What best of revealed e book do you need?

Some self-publishing offerings offer confined or no choice in how your published e-book is probably produced. CreateSpace, as an example, permits you to supply paperback books most effective, while Lulu gives various binding alternatives. Decide what you need after which study your options.

How an lousy lot do you want to rate in your ebook?

This would possibly likely have an effect on your publishing selections – ebooks are sincere as there are not any printing charges to maintain in mind – really determine at the price and study the services and shops that guide your desire. On Amazon there may be a minimal promoting rate of £0.Seventy five/$0.99 however you may make your e-book available out of your very personal net web site or Smashwords with out value. Print on Demand (POD) books might also additionally have a higher constant with duplicate manufacturing fee than printing multiple copies, if you need to preserve the fee low you can want to undergo in mind paying prematurely for a print run.

How masses time do you want to allocate to selling your e-book?

You may additionally additionally revel in the selling and advertising and marketing issue of self-ebook or you could pick out to allocate some time to writing. Some self-publishing offerings provide you with inclusive promotions. Whilst you may select out to put up to all the available structures there may be a few rules, e.G. In case you pick out to sign on into KDP Select (Kindle) you can not offer your ebook available on the market some location else.

Publishing an e-book

In modern years there has been an e-book revolution; readers are consuming ebooks at an first-rate fee and there's no signal of this trend slowing. Readers can calm down with their ereader, browse books online, make a purchase and start studying inside mins. We stay in a direct society; on the identical time as a customer makes a purchase they want their item now.

Publishing an ebook might be the quickest, best and cheapest way to get your e-book in front of your capability readers. There are many awesome benefits to publishing an e-book; royalties are better than for revealed books (specially due to tons much less high priced manufacturing and shipping prices), readers have immediately get right of entry to to their purchases and publishing is short and clean.

Ebooks may be read on a computer, laptop, pill, ereader and mobile cellphone. Just don't forget the capability readers you have to be had to you. With ereaders now available with net get right of entry to and a full-size kind of apps, essentially setting them into the tablet magnificence, they'll be handiest going to emerge as more well-known.

Ebooks have a propensity to be pretty priced, even reasonably-priced; the result is that readers will supply little notion to developing that £2.Ninety nine buy probably in the equal way they supply little concept whilst identifying to shop for a cup of coffee. For the author this means extra books sold.

With a number of publishers imparting publishing, vending and distribution offerings free of charge, two famous ones are Amazon's KDP and Smashwords, you may truely positioned up and sell these days.

Publishing with Amazon's KDP offers you with up to 70% royalties and some free promotional pastime along aspect emails to readers recommending books primarily based on their preceding purchases and a "clients furthermore sold" characteristic.

Publishing with Smashwords gives you with as plenty as 80 five% royalties and moreover offers the opportunity to make your e-book available on Apple iBookstore, Barnes and Noble and distinct on-line outlets.

If you choice to promote your e-book as an e-book thru your private distribution channels you may format your ebook as a pdf record (see bankruptcy four) and sell through your very very own website or thru an internet keep of virtual merchandise.

Publishing an e-book has a whole lot to provide each the latest and experienced author. Now is the time to benefit from this digital revolution.

Publishing a published ebook

For a writer there may be now not some thing pretty like protecting a physical replica of your e-book to your arms. Even better is seeing copies of your book on the shelves of bookstores. There are many advantages to publishing a posted ebook; you can use features that might not display efficiently on ereaders, e.G. Tables.

You manage a whole lot of the formatting along side textual content kind and length. You can sell your ebook in locations no longer ideal to the sale of ebooks which include your education sports or excessive avenue shops; and, as with ebooks, you may put up without rate.

The charge of producing a broadcast e book is higher than an e-book so that you will need to endure in mind your pricing approach. It is flawlessly OK to fee precise costs for posted and ebook versions of the identical ebook. In truth there may be a bonus to this – readers see the e-book at a substantially decrease rate and understand that they may be getting first rate charge for cash.

There are numerous techniques to method publishing a broadcast ebook.

Chapter 10: Print On Demand (Pod)

This is a quick, smooth and frequently free manner to region up a e-book; as you do no longer need to put money into a print run you may moreover check the marketplace.

There are many advantages to POD which encompass no storage problems, no upfront bills for print runs and the functionality to alternate the content fabric of your ebook with out looking for previous stock to be presented.

The vital downside is that printing costs can be better than different techniques this means that you can want to charge a higher fee to your e-book or be prepared to take a decrease profits margin.

CreateSpace (Amazon) provides writers with a loose issuer which includes advertising and distribution. They will preserve an amount of money from the sale of every replica supplied; you could set the e-book fee for that reason and so determine your earnings.

Lulu is each other popular POD carrier that is simple to apply; they will furthermore promote your ebook from their website. Lulu has the extra advantage of imparting you more than a few binding and paper options.

Both Amazon and Lulu have greater distribution channels you may purchase into.

Print run

Commissioning an extended print run (1000+ copies) can significantly lessen the price of every e book. You can each use a self-publishing organization or arrange the printing yourself thru a nearby or expert printer.

Which self-publishing carrier?

Amazon's KDP – a unfastened to use carrier that allows you to position up your ebook and make it available throughout all of Amazon's territories; they manage earnings and distribution and offer precise royalty alternatives based totally mostly on your pricing. KDP furthermore have various promotional equipment that help developing your income in conjunction with a "clients additionally furnished" phase.

If you join up into KDP Select you may sell your e-book as unfastened for 5 days in every ninety and you may earn income whenever your ebook is borrowed with the useful resource of Amazon Prime people.

Smashwords – a loose to use provider imparting various distribution channels collectively with iBookstore and Barnes and Noble. They will control income and distribution and provide royalty alternatives primarily based on distribution channels.

Lulu — a famous unfastened to use POD organisation that offers you, the author, various binding options. Lulu is a famous POD service that lets in you to create a posted ebook that meets your necessities. Lulu presents pretty quite a number options which includes paper grade, paperback or hardback, coloration or black and white. You can choose out to pay for the worldwide gather opportunity if you need to make your ebook available to bookstores.

Amazon's CreateSpace — each different loose to apply POD provider that prints your e book as a paperback and makes it to be had on Amazon. They also offer expanded distribution channels for which there may be a cost.

Self-publishing agencies - a number of agencies provide self-publishing applications. It is vital to hold in mind all components of printing and promoting a posted book which will determine on the high-quality bundle for you.

There are some excellent self-publishing businesses available in addition to a few who rate quite a few cash for a terrible issuer (vanity publishers). Good agencies will work with you to offer expert recommendation and services ensuing in a bundle that is tailored to fulfill your needs.

Typical applications embody editing, cowl layout, ISBN, ebook conversion, selling to booksellers, coping with storage and distribution, and printing an agreed variety of your e-book.

It is profitable spending a while getting hints, touring the organisation premises and analyzing samples of discovered books in advance than deciding on which self-publishing corporation to apply. Always test the settlement earlier than signing.

Managing the e-book method yourself - you could of direction manage the whole gadget your self and buy in the offerings you need from separate belongings. You may additionally even determine to set up your personal publishing agency. If you choose this route preserve in thoughts the time you can need to make investments coping with the publishing system, and earnings and distribution. Of route this will be the start of an entire new organisation, one you experience as plenty as writing.

The choice is yours. Decide at the incredible approach for you and then start getting prepared your ebook for ebook.

3 - Preparing your ebook for e-book – crowning glory

You have written your ebook and need to make it to be had to readers as fast as feasible. Just in advance than you post you want to complete some responsibilities to make sure it seems extremely good, meets any publishing necessities and is successfully promoted.

You need to edit your e book, create a pick out, create a cowl, write an define and blurb, write the front and back do not forget and then layout your paintings to fulfill the requirements of your preferred guide method.

If you've got found the stairs in Write it! - a manner to install writing your e-book in 30 hours or lots less, you're prepared to visit the subsequent bankruptcy and layout your e-book.

Create a call

A excellent perceive will seize the eye of readers; that is step one in the direction of creating a purchase.

A cautiously crafted identify will encourage search engines like google and yahoo to propel your ebook to the number one web web page of include looking for outcomes. Note that the majority of folks that are in search of online for merchandise do not look beyond web page 3; if your ebook appears after this a reader might also additionally moreover in no way recognise it exists. If readers do no longer see it they may now not purchase it.

Titles are crucial, many readers will make a purchase based totally totally on the call on my own, this is mainly right for non-fiction books. If you have got were given written a fiction ebook you'll be innovative at the side of your grow to be aware of however make certain you never deceive your reader; preserve in mind you want them to shop for your future titles. If you have written a non-fiction ebook your identify want to mirror the problem depend range and help search engines like google like google locating your book on the same time as someone desires to buy a e-book in your trouble rely.

One of the pleasant tactics to approach developing a become aware of for every fiction and non-fiction books is to create a brief become privy to, which is probably contemporary, accompanied by the usage of a sub-name, which need to be descriptive. Think approximately the terms and phrases that ability readers can also type proper proper into a seek engine to find out the type of ebook you have got were given were given written – try and consist of the ones phrases and terms into your sub-name. You can determine whether or now not or no longer to encompass the sub-emerge as aware of on the cover of your e-book, however make certain you encompass it anywhere else to maximise impact.

Consider the ones examples of titles with sub-titles. Both are pretty brief despite the fact that you can see how the sub-find out may enhance search engine optimization.

Steam – a statistics of steam engines in trains and device inside the course of the nineteenth century.

Life (Thriller set on Death Row).

If you are publishing your e-book as an e-book or the usage of POD it is simple to exchange the call if you find out the ebook is not making the preferred profits.

Chapter 11: Create A Cowl

Never choose a ebook via using its cover! Of path that is precisely what every body does. Your cover desires to be captivating and appearance professional. Your cowl want to trap the reader and encourage them to take a look at your description or blurb.

Many writers pick to outsource their cover layout; you can use on-line offerings, a close-by fashion fashion designer, or strive your neighborhood university and observe if any college students would really like a live task. Always deliver an extensive brief to make sure the duvet presentations the concern and content cloth of your e-book due to the reality your cowl is a key promoting device.

A free possibility is to use on-line cowl creators which can be available with some on line publishing offerings, e.G. CreateSpace, those include smooth to apply templates and get admission to to immoderate high-quality pics. If you're the use of a self-publishing enterprise agency they will provide cowl design as part of the bundle.

If you have got the layout capabilities or a constrained rate range then create the cover your self the use of image-editing software software; there's amazing software available at no cost. You can take your non-public images to use collectively along with your format or purchase pictures on-line for an inexpensive fee; make sure any sold photos are royalty loose.

If you are taking the DIY approach the crucial issue to growing an attractive cowl is to preserve it clean:

- Use no greater than 3 taken into consideration considered one of a type font kinds.

- Use pictures that represent the general topic, hassle depend wide variety, placing or characters of your ebook.

- Ensure that any text may be examine over the chosen photo. Of course you may determine not to use photos in any respect.

- Ensure the threshold of your e book is darkish, add a skinny, darkish border if vital. This will ensure your ebook sticks out even as displayed on-line as it is probably to be displayed in competition to a white historical past.

- Image period is important for each epublishing and printing. It is critical to check the necessities of every author. For epublishing a photograph width of a minimum 1400 pixels with a ratio of one:1.6 works nicely. For discovered books your picture duration can be primarily based absolutely mostly on your e-book duration so pick out your e-book length first and set your photograph duration therefore. For revealed books your cowl will embody the once more and determination.

- As a totally last check ensure your cover appears appealing in greyscale.

Keep notes about your cover format as you may want to recreate it; it is frequently easier to recreate your cover than to make modifications to an gift picture.

Note: in case you intend to use a web cowl creator it's far useful to prepare your pix and produce a mock-up of your cowl earlier than you publish.

Write a blurb and outline

The purpose of each the blurb and outline is to ensure readers make a purchase; after studying the ones they'll each decide no longer to shop for or upload the e-book to their basket. These are your excessive advertising gear – use them well.

Generally the blurb goes on the back of your discovered out e-book and the outline may be displayed to your e book's on-line profits pages. Whilst the identical textual content may be used for both you'll be lacking a massive marketing opportunity in case you do now not make tremendous use of an outline. Both can be used on special promotional material - press release, weblog, internet site, advert or leaflet.

The blurb is mostly a paragraph orin period and is used to trap the reader to study more e.G. "Following the dying of her father Mary returns to her family home to sell the residence and tie up unfastened ends. Little did she apprehend the lengthy held secrets she should find out that might rock her understanding of who she end up and located her lifestyles in risk."

The description is frequently longer and gives extra data about your ebook; it is able to encompass the blurb. As the define is used on line - shops, your internet web site and evaluate web sites - it is vital to use as many key phrases and phrases that is probably used by those looking for a ebook like yours. "Are you trying to find to start a domestic-based enterprise," "collecting teddy bears." Using applicable seek engine quality terms in your description receives your e-book displayed even as readers are seeking out your form of ebook.

If your capability readers in no way see your ebook they will never purchase it; the outline is one in every of your simplest promotional gear. Spend a while thinking about what a reader may input when looking for a e-book like yours; obviously do now not deceive your readers however accumulating teddy bears may also encompass a connection with antiques, toys, dolls homes, offers, car boot sales, eBay, days out, journeying historic houses and extra.

Your writing have to stand out – the blurb will entice the reader to study greater, the description is a sales web page to persuade them to hit the "Buy Now" button.

Write your the the front do not forget

Front consider is the more data that is going at the start of your ebook. If you are publishing each an e-book and a published ebook, or a the use of a number of precise publishing offerings, you can need barely special versions to satisfy minimal requirements. Front rely must encompass:

Title – each the principle end up privy to and sub-call

Author – your call or pen call

Publisher – each your name, your pen call or a creator call in case you set up a publishing company

Copyright - use the picture or the word copyright discovered through owner of the copyright (author call/pen name) and year of first guide

ISBN – required for published books, at the same time as this isn't vital for ebooks you could need one to sell via a few on line shops

Kindle or Smashwords Edition - for ebooks you could require the ones terms relying at the publishing provider decided on.

Take a check the start of this ebook to look how little is absolutely required.

You might also additionally moreover determine to embody extra the the front take into account which includes a prison assertion, acknowledgements, dedications, credit score, foreword or version amount.

Note: If you put up to Amazon's Kindle or Smashwords then your ebook will have a in addition promotional device – "See interior" or "Sample" – some of pages may be made available for readers to preview and down load. Try now not to litter up the to be had pattern pages with the the front keep in mind variety; you need to use this promotional tool to its wonderful benefit and ensure that what readers see encourages them to shop for. Once you've got got met the minimum necessities for the

the the front bear in mind then you may select out to region the whole lot else in the back of your book.

Add once more don't forget

You may additionally additionally choice to function additional material on the give up of your e-book; this will embody fabric that enables your e-book inclusive of a word list. It is most beneficial for selling exceptional books you have got written, your net internet site on-line, blog, social media records and distinctive offerings you offer.

Create promotional pages for every of your books, you can use the description and critiques for this, encompass how to buy statistics, this want to embody a clickable hyperlink in an ebook or the overall internet internet page deal with in discovered books, in no manner use clickable accomplice links as a few shops do no longer permit the ones. Remove any charge info as you could alternate the ones over the years.

Promote your next ebook, even if you have no longer yet written it. It is a high-quality idea to offer a manual date as this offers readers a few component to live up for, creates anticipation, and additionally offers you a last date. Once you have got have been given published your subsequent e-book undergo in mind to replace this promotional page to consist of the new records.

Promote books by using the use of specific writers; this may be a reciprocal affiliation wherein moreover they sell your art work. In most times you aren't in competition with wonderful writers, human beings buy greater of what they pick in preference to selecting definitely one ebook from a class. Promoting on this manner can align you with distinct a success writers.

Create a web page to sell your unique sports activities sports together together with your internet internet page, weblog and your business company, as an example you'll be a consultant, traveler speaker or trainer. Give human beings a reason to study your weblog, tell them the blessings, e.G. "I will publish statistics of e-book promotions right here" or "hints and recommendations on strategies to make more money". As earlier than upload a link or provide net web site statistics.

These pages are an outstanding opportunity in case you want to sell yourself – make use of them.

Set the rate

Price topics. Price may additionally have a big effect on each profits and profits earned from both this ebook and distinctive books you write; it can be useful to have a pricing method that could embody price changes at some stage in the lifespan of your ebook.

Price too low and readers might also moreover apprehend your e-book as having little fee. Price too excessive and you may restrict your marketplace.

Consider your goals. Do you need to sell excessive volumes of books with a view to get your name recognised and therefore create a devoted following to be able to be prepared to pay better expenses for your future books, or do you need to maximize your income from this one ebook?

Your goals can also exchange sooner or later of the lifespan of your e-book. Often writers lessen the price of a e-book when they publish a new e-book, probably the following in a chain; readers purchase the primary at a discounted fee after which cross on to shop for the following ebook at a higher charge. This is a way that is a fulfillment and boom your general ebook profits and earnings.

There might be a minimum fee you want to rate, even though you will be prepared to make quick term losses that allows you to sell this or different books. If you are publishing a published ebook you'll fee based mostly on your manufacturing fees (collectively with company employer charges), and then upload an quantity which will become your income.

If you have were given invested in a print run you could also need to do not forget how many books you're in all likelihood to sell initially, use this as the premise for shielding your manufacturing expenses. If you keep in mind you studied you will with out trouble promote 100 and fifty books then fee to cowl all your costs with the sale of one hundred fifty books, you start growing a make the most of the sale of e-book range 151.

If you're publishing an e-book you may want to test the publishing provider/keep tips. If you publish to Amazon's Kindle using KDP you ought to have a minimum fee of £zero.Seventy five/$zero.Ninety nine but, to benefit 70% royalties, you may need to rate at among £1.Forty nine/$2.Ninety nine - £6.Ninety nine/$nine.Ninety nine. When promoting on Amazon you can't provide your e-book at a inexpensive fee some place else. Amazon do not let you positioned up with a zero fee but you can use their selling scheme to offer your e-book freed from price for 5 days in ninety. Some writers employ Amazon's price healthy; they offer their book for gratis elsewhere and then wait until Amazon additionally gadgets the rate to zero. Think cautiously earlier than taking this technique as you'll be in breach of Amazon's terms and conditions.

The manufacturing prices for found out books may be higher than for ebooks, because of this you could determine to charge unique expenses for the only of a kind codecs. There can be a bonus to doing this because the reader will perceive the e-book as being high-quality fee if appreciably less costly than the printed model.

Over time you can pick out to test with the price to maximize earnings. For example if you sell a thousand copies of your e-book for £zero.Ninety nine at 35% royalties you earn a hint under £350. If you sell a hundred copies at £6.Ninety nine at 70% royalties then your profits may be honestly beneath £500. Get this proper and you can maximize your income.

Edit

Your textual content have to be as near mistakes free as feasible even as you submit, however if you are publishing an ebook or the use of POD and you, or your proofreader, leave out some thing you can commonly make adjustments and republish at a later date.

It is beneficial to make numerous passes of your e book, every with a one in all a kind cause; this lets in you to consciousness at the venture in location of skimming through the text as if you are a reader.

Read your art work aloud, this could assist your be conscious wherein the phrases don't float.

Check for needless adverbs and adjectives, get rid of them, and if crucial look for a stronger verb or noun e.G. Instead of "he ran very rapid" try "he sprinted". You can use a phrase listing for this.

Check spelling – in case you are uncertain use a dictionary, or trade the word. Ensure you test for common misspellings – there, their, they're. Spell-check might not pick out those up.

Check punctuation – out of vicinity apostrophes are the bane of readers' lives. If unsure rewrite the sentence.

Check all hyperlinks in ebooks – ensure they artwork.

It is useful to include the net cope with in full in addition to a "click here" hyperlink. This will assist readers discover the internet website or web web page.

Check records – if you are using proper records then check it with as a minimum 3 belongings.

Chapter 12: Save A Draw Close Duplicate

Save a replica of your e-book and get in touch with it xxxfinaledited.Doc.

When your e-book is finished store a Master duplicate as a study simplest report to make sure you do no longer accidently overwrite at some level within the formatting for ebook machine.

If, at a later degree, you need to make a few changes, e.G. You discover a spelling mistakes, make the adjustments in this Master after which begin the approach of formatting for guide once more to make sure all copies are the identical.

You are truly organized to layout and post your ebook.

four - Preparing your ebook for ebook - formatting

To ensure your e-book appears exceptional on all ereaders and in print you need to layout it to meet the necessities of your preferred publishing approach and to make certain the contents of your book are efficaciously displayed or observed.

To layout your e book you could use any phrase-processor that allows you to store as report, pdf and html. This want now not contain costly software program purchases; every LibreOffice and OpenOffice are loose to down load and do the system properly. If you want to transform your book into distinct codecs, for instance ePub, you will discover on line conversion tools, regularly those are supplied via way of the self-publishing business enterprise.

Note: if you intend to sell your ebook out of your internet web site or thru a digital products preserve you will probably want to layout your e-book as a pdf. If that is the case have a look at the commands for formatting a published ebook, the pdf is designed to be study on line further to found out. Set your internet page period to

A4 or to a contemporary print paper duration.

Formatting your ebook

One of the blessings of ereaders is that clients have full-size control over the way text is displayed; this consists of font length, kind and coloration. This approach you have to create a record that consists of minimum formatting to ensure your e-book appears incredible at the same time as have a look at.

The conversion method from phrase-processed document to ereader layout can also furthermore forget approximately some of your implemented formatting; in truth awesome ereader codecs can also additionally behave in awesome methods. Your e-book needs to look amazing even though all the formatting is eliminated. To make certain your e-book seems exceptional you want to take a look at one rule – Keep it Simple.

Styles – many ereaders manual patterns, in truth a few conversions appoint them however, you want to keep those simple. Use Normal, Heading 1 and Heading 2; you can use Heading 3 if desired but any more than this could have a negative effect at the conversion. Modify the patterns if essential to fit your wishes. Set Normal to Arial font period 12, Heading 1 (for financial ruin headings) to Arial font size 14, bold and targeted, Heading 2 (for subheadings) to font period 12 and formidable. Bold and align centre normally display as formatted. Do now not workout coloration as this can now not display on black and white ereaders.

Font kind, period and color – you could observe formatting without delay to the textual content, continuously use a large font type inclusive of Arial, Times New Roman or Garamond, and recall the purchaser can alternate this to healthy their possibilities. Keep the same font type at some stage in your e book and outstanding trade the dimensions for monetary disaster headings and sub-headings. Colour need to be set to black or computerized.

Emphasis – italics, bold and underline are usually preserved. Leave those to your text however make certain the text is easy to observe if those are removed or modified.

Spacing among words – use one location best amongst every phrase, this consists of spacing after a complete save you. Additional areas can be removed within the conversion manner. A quick way to updateareas with one space is to use your phrase-processor's discover and update feature; within the discover container press the distance bartimes, inside the update field press the spacebar as fast as. Select replace all and the hobby is finished.

Paragraphs – decide to each use an indent at the begin of every new paragraph OR a line area amongst paragraphs; do now not use each for the same paragraph. Typically an indent is used for fiction and a line area is used for non-fiction but the preference is yours. If making a decision to apply an indent you should use the first line indent formatting feature, do not use the gap bar or tabs. Select all of your text, pick out out format paragraph and set first line indent to zero.5cm.

Note: if you have a line place after a economic ruin heading you have to put off the indent from that first paragraph.

Bullets and automatic numbering – those might not be supported on the ereader so eliminate automatic bullets and numbering and replace humans with manually entered numbers.

Return/Enter key – on the identical time as you press the go back key you begin a contemporary paragraph and paragraph formatting e.G. First line indent, is executed. However some ebook conversions will ignore all but the first tough return and remove any line spacing you have got have been given created. If you need to location more line regions between text use Shift+Return to create a pressured line wreck. If you need to maintain any paragraph formatting, e.G. First line indent, then use the Return key on its private for the final line place.

Alignment – except textual content formatted as targeted, e.G. Bankruptcy headings, all textual content must be left aligned or justified. The ereader could have a default show putting which, in a few instances, can be controlled with the beneficial resource of the individual. It is in all likelihood that the ereader will show the textual content as justified.

Tabs – many ereaders do not beneficial aid them; use the first line indent characteristic to indent if required.

Tables – the ones are not currently supported by using the use of manner of many ereaders. If you've got created a desk that is critical for your ebook, reproduce and insert it as an photograph.

Columns – those may not show successfully on maximum ereaders. It is higher to take away the columns however if you be given as actual with that preserving the columns is essential then reproduce and insert as an photo. Aim to hold the text content material fabric material in pix at a minimum as you can lose some of the clarity.

Page breaks – the ones paintings on a few ereaders and are ignored with the beneficial useful resource of others. If you are publishing to more than one ereaders and do no longer need to create separate files for each one you could overcome this thru setting an internet web page ruin straight away after the last sentence of a bankruptcy after which placing a maximum of 4 pressured line breaks in advance than beginning the subsequent financial disaster. If the net page breaks is recognized then the subsequent bankruptcy will begin partway down the following web web page, that is flawlessly ideal and occasionally preferred. If the net web page damage is unnoticed there may be an low-fee area some of thechapters.

Headers and footers – get rid of those alongside element any internet internet web page numbering.

Line spacing - set line spacing between 1 and 1.Five, as with one-of-a-kind formatting this will be controlled via the usage of the ereader. Set the sooner than and after paragraph spacing to 0.

Emphasis – use ambitious, italics and/or underline with consistency.

Colour – some ereaders are black and white only, others supply the character manipulate over textual content color. Use black super for textual content and make sure snap shots are clear when displayed in greyscale.

Images - make sure pix appearance pinnacle even as displayed in greyscale. You can also want to consider record length of the photographs, e.G. Whilst publishing to Kindle the maximum photograph duration is 127KB.

Note: sooner or later of the conversion technique your pics may be stored as separate documents, you truely need to don't forget this if you are saving or shifting documents into new places on your laptop – bear in mind to transport the image files and preserve any folder structure.

Links – the ones are supported as long as the ereader facilitates net browsing and is set up to the net. It can be useful to offer the net address in addition to a click on on proper right here opportunity. Test all links to make sure they work efficiently.

Step via step - formatting your ebook

1) Open your edited document. Save the file as xxxfinalebookformatted.Document. Do not overwrite your edited grasp as you can want it later. Save your artwork frequently.

2) Add your e-book the the the front matter to the start of your e-book.

three) Change text to a desired font kind and size, e.G. Arial, length 12, both without delay or thru the use of patterns.

four) Apply font length and emphasis formatting as required, e.G. Chapter headings, both right away or using styles.

five) Set line spacing to among 1 and 1.Five, if required set first line indent to 0.5cm, set spacing in advance than and after paragraph to 0 and alignment to left aligned or justified (paragraph formatting).

6) Remove headers, footers and net page numbering.

7) Turn on show/cover (Pilcrow) button to reveal all non-printing characters.

eight) Remove all tabs, replace with first line indent if required.

nine) Remove greater areas amongst phrases.

10) Remove automated bullets and numbering; replace manually as required.

eleven) Remove greater tough returns and update with mild/forced returns in which a couple of line place is wanted.

12) Remove first line indent from first paragraph of each chapter if you have entered a line place among economic catastrophe heading and the primary paragraph.

thirteen) Check net page breaks are located right now after the closing word or punctuation mark of each financial ruin. If required upload more line regions using a gentle/forced flow once more at the give up of every monetary disaster.

14) Centre economic damage headings if required.

15) Add and take a look at internal and outside links.

16) Save.

This document will now be used to publish your e-book. As unique offerings require exquisite document codecs at this degree keep as a report document, you'll convert at the publishing degree.

You are honestly equipped to publish your e-book.

Chapter 13: Formatting Your Posted Ebook

Publishing a broadcast e book opens up substantial markets to writers; bookshops can stock and promote your e-book and you can sell copies at your talks or education periods.

If you will sell through online stores which includes Amazon then the quickest and cheapest (no in advance costs) way to get commenced out is to apply a Print on Demand (POD) company that prints and binds each duplicate as it's miles ordered. The production price in keeping with e-book is better than commissioning a print run however you do no longer need to spend money on printing and storing more than one copies.

Most POD services pick or require the ebook to be formatted as a pdf file. This gives you massive manage over the way the e-book seems as you can employ greater formatting features. It is however essential to comply with submission necessities, which specifically relate to trim period and margins, else your e-book can be rejected or won't print efficiently.

Before you begin you need to determine on the dimensions of your ebook; you may then installation the precise web web page/trim duration. It is better to use a huge length, there are various, as some shops might not stock books of a non-popular length. Also test any sizing constraints regarding specific options such as paper colour and binding.

I might also want to advise downloading and the use of templates to be had from POD services collectively with Amazon's CreateSpace or Lulu. These templates will will let you import your text (replica and paste) to a template this is installation with the proper internet web page period and margins; some templates encompass steerage on content cloth and formatting, e.G. The the front depend and font sorts.

170

Take a take a look at the ones available at https://www.Createspace.Com/en/network /scientific medical doctors/DOC-1323

Font type – because of the fact that may be a discovered e-book you may select the font type, however you continue to need to maintain this smooth. You additionally want to test that the font will embed effectively, the font is freely available so you can use and that it's going to appearance suitable while revealed; some fonts appearance exquisite on display display screen but lousy at the same time as located; stay with the tried and examined at the side of Times New Roman, Arial or Garamond. Generally speakme a serif font kind is higher for discovered books but sans serif can artwork nicely for more youthful kids.

Font period – set to eleven or 12, do a sample print to appearance how this looks. You can set bankruptcy headings to a bigger font duration, 14 works properly but you could want to test with up to length sixteen.

Note: when you installation your record using a POD provider you could discover that there may be a slight model at the determined out font duration as the pages can be "healthy to web web page" if there isn't an actual net page period in shape.

Styles – the settings are preserved while changing to pdf. Keep patterns smooth and use handiest famous font kinds. Set up patterns in your body textual content, monetary ruin headings, sub-headings and a few different blocks of textual content that require a specific look.

Alignment – Most discovered books are simply justified. If you choose you could left align, this could enhance clarity in books designed for younger kids.

Drop capitals – decide if you would like to apply drop capitals on the start of every financial disaster, the ones can be preserved on the equal time as converting to pdf.

Line spacing – set this between 1 and 1.2. This seems expert and allows keep charge down as an increase in line spacing equals extra pages. Set spacing in advance than and after paragraphs to 0.

Page breaks – insert web net web page breaks on the cease of every financial ruin and everywhere else you determined an internet page destroy will enhance format.

Paragraphs – decide to every use an indent at the start of each new paragraph OR a line area amongst paragraphs; do not use each for the same paragraph. Typically an indent is used for fiction and a line region is used for non-fiction but the preference is yours. If making a decision to apply an indent you ought to use the number one line indent formatting feature, do not use the space bar or tabs. Select all your text, select format paragraph and set first line indent to zero.5cm.

Note: if you have a line area after a bankruptcy heading you have to do away with the indent from that first paragraph.

Margins — set as required, this could maximum in all likelihood be decided thru your publishing enterprise; test their tips or use their template. Remember the inner margin will need to be slightly wider than the outer margin to allow for binding, that is referred to as the gutter. You will need to mirror margins as you are printing on each facets of the paper. As a guiding precept set the outer, pinnacle and bottom margin to 0.5in and the inner margin to 0.75in, this includes an quantity for the gutter.

Note: measurements are given in inches as this has a bent to be utilized by the agency.

Headers, footers and net internet web page numbers — you're able to use headers, footers and internet web page numbering in published books, in truth you need to continually consist of internet page numbers. You can also want to encompass the chapter name within the header, in all likelihood the author name in the footer, and you could use sturdy strains to interrupt up the header from the frame of the textual content. Have a observe some examples of books that make suitable use of headers and footers and then decide the manner you need yours to appearance.

Tables – pdf files assist tables, make certain they healthful on the net web page if you have reduced the internet web web page duration right down to your desired e-book length.

Tabs – the ones are supported even as changing to pdf, as with tables ensure those although look right at the identical time as the web net page length is reduced.

Columns – you're able to use columns with a broadcast e-book; cause for every column to be at least 5 phrases large, till a listing, as this improves clarity.

Bullets and numbering – you can use computerized numbering and upload bullet points for your e-book.

Images – make sure your picture will print virtually whilst resized to fit your net web page or the gap allocated to it. If you are not printing in shade then convert your photograph to greyscale in advance than you insert it into your e-book.

Colour – books may be determined in coloration but this may upload to the rate. If making a decision to print in black and white or greyscale then change font colour to black or grey and convert pics to greyscale.

Links – as that could be a posted ebook hyperlinks will need to be removed, you should replace any click on proper here links with the overall internet deal with, e.G. https://www.Google.Co.United u . S . A ., you may moreover want to reword the textual content explaining the hyperlink.

Step by using way of the usage of step - formatting your posted e-book

1) Open your hold close report and hold as xxxformatforprint.Document (you could convert to a pdf on the end).

2) Set the internet page length as required and set your margins to zero.5in for top, backside and outside facet and 0.75in for the indoors aspect (to be positive). You should then replicate margins as you will be printing on every aspects of the paper.

OR

1) Open a ebook duration template and maintain as xxxformatforprint.Document.

2) Import/duplicate and paste the textual content from your grasp record into the template.

AND

three) Add your front and back depend.

Note: you can require an ISBN for found out books.

four) Add web page breaks wherein desired.

5) Use styles or at once have a look at formatting in your text, e.G. Font size, kind and emphasis, make certain consistency of formatting for frame textual content, headings, charges and thoughts.

6) Add headers, footers and page numbers.

7) Set line spacing amongst 1 and 1.2.

eight) Set alignment to left align or absolutely justified.

9) Centre text as required, e.G. Bankruptcy headings.

10) Add greater emphasis (italics, formidable, underline) as required.

eleven) Add bullet factors and numbering, format those as required.

12) Check pics are efficiently placed.

13) Remove any links and make sure net addresses are written in full.

14) Save your modifications.

15) Save as a pdf report making sure that you embed images and fonts.

16) Open your new report in a pdf reader to make sure all textual content and formatting is displayed as intended. Make modifications if required.

Your ebook is now equipped to publish.

five - Publishing

You now have a formatted manuscript prepared to post. Unless you have got a specific purpose to provide a posted ebook first I may advise publishing an e-book. This offers you the possibility to look your e-book available to shop for in a only some hours or perhaps in only some mins.

Publishing to Amazon's Kindle using KDP

Amazon's Kindle is the market leader in e-readers, books can be read on a Kindle and Kindle apps allowing readers to buy and test books on their ereader, cell cellular cellphone, tablet, or pc. Once you have were given got long gone thru the e book approach your e-book will generally be available on the Amazon net site indoors 12 hours.

KDP allows you to feature and put up from masses of codecs in conjunction with record, html, pdf, txt, and specific formats. It can be useful to transform your file to the share layout as, on the time of writing, this lets in you to thoroughly take a look at your ebook on a Kindle or Kindle app previous to e-book, this makes it easier to look any formatting mistakes. Mobipocket Creator can be used to transform your ebook into the share layout.

If making a decision on you can skip this next stage and pass right away to the following segment - Publishing with KDP.

Step thru step – growing a percentage report the usage of Mobipocket Creator

1) Download and deploy a reproduction of Mobipocket Creator from www.Mobipocket.Com

Note: that is presently only to be had for PCs.

2) Open your formatted for e-book record - xxxfinalebookformatted.Doc - and shop as a Web Page Filtered or html document. You will need it in this format whether or not or now not you operate Mobipocket Creator first or skip immediately to KDP.

3) Open Mobipocket Creator.

4) From the list beneath Import From Existing File select out HTML Document.

five) Browse for your saved html report, select out and click on on on Import.

6) Click on Cover Image, positioned inside the list on the left. Click Add cowl picture.

7) Browse for and select out the image.

8) Important - scroll to the lowest at the net net web page and click on Update.

nine) Using the alternatives on the left facet of the show display screen you could add a table of contents and metadata but those aren't crucial. If you pick out out to function metadata test every field is stuffed in successfully as a few facts have to be entered in a selected way, e.G. The author call is entered as surname, first name.

10) Scroll to the bottom of the display and click on on Update.

11) From the icons along the top of the display click Build and then Build.

12) If you get any mistakes messages have a study those and correct. The maximum commonplace one takes region because of the reality you haven't clicked on Update after deciding on a cowl photograph or collectively with metadata.

13) When Build has finished click on on on Open Folder and then OK.

14) You now have a % report ready to replicate for your Kindle content fabric folder.

15) If you're using your laptop and feature downloaded Kindle for PC you may have a folder referred to as My Kindle Content; replica the % record into this folder.

OR

15) If you need to duplicate the file onto a Kindle, be a part of it to your laptop via a USB port and copy the p.C file into the Kindle's document folder.

AND

16) Turn for your Kindle or open Kindle for PC and your ebook might be to be had to take a look at, don't worry if the cover isn't displayed, this could be awesome while posted through KDP.

17) Thoroughly test via your ebook and search for formatting errors.

18) Correct formatting errors to your formatted for e-book Word file; any spelling errors must be corrected inside the Master similarly to the formatted model. Save as Web Page Filtered or html and convert to p.C the usage of Mobipocket Creator.

19) Repeat till you're satisfied with the manner your e-book is displayed.

You are simply organized to place as tons as Amazon Kindle save the use of KDP.

www.ingramcontent.com/pod-product-compliance
Lightning Source LLC
Chambersburg PA
CBHW070609220426
43635CB00030B/459